On the SMALL SIDE

Photos & Stories

CATHRYN WELLNER

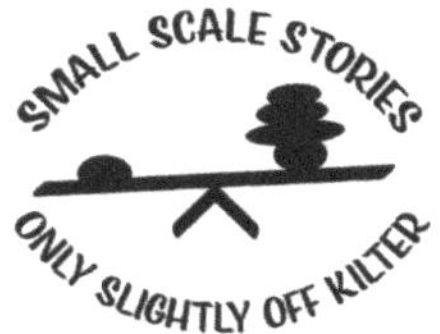

Small Scale Stories #10
Espoir Press
British Columbia 2019

Espoir Press
1002 - 1128 Sunset Drive
Kelowna, British Columbia
Canada V1Y 9W7

On the Small Side (Small Scale Stories #10)

ISBN 978-1-988760-18-6

Credits

Fonts used on cover and some interior pages: Canvas, Saltash, Sun Kissed. Font used in stories: Bw Surco. Logo font: Ed's Market. Graphics on dedication page are from Zeppelin Graphics. All other fonts and graphic elements are licensed through DesignCuts.

Text and photographs by Cathryn Wellner. The book was designed in Photoshop.

Thank you to the creative people who designed the unique fonts and elements incorporated in this book. I continually learn from you.

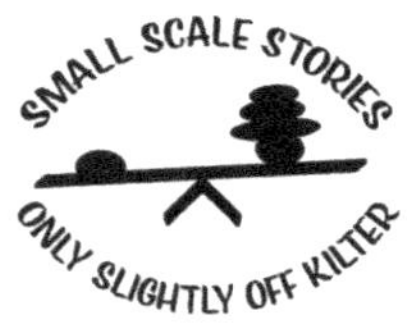

SMALL BUT MIGHTY

If you ever feel too small to make a difference, consider the burr, whose seeds grab your socks and will not let go. Instead of just being irritated by them, Swiss inventor George de Mestral examined them under a microscope. He discovered they were covered with tiny hooks. That led him to invent Velcro. The burrs live on, traveling to new places on socks and fur. Their imitators pop up on shoes, bags, clothing, and anywhere fasteners are needed.

Burrs, Velcro, and even socks and fur are all connected. We may not always be a happy family, but we are all related. John Muir said it beautifully in his book, *Nature Writings*: "When we try to pick out anything by itself, we find it hitched to everything else in the Universe."

You and I, my friend, are cousins. So is the duck who watches to see if you've brought her seed. So is the magical Japanese maple in the nearby garden, where the fairies dance. So is the mechanical crane who admires his reflection in a wall of windows.

How you treat your relatives matters. You create ripples that change whatever they touch.

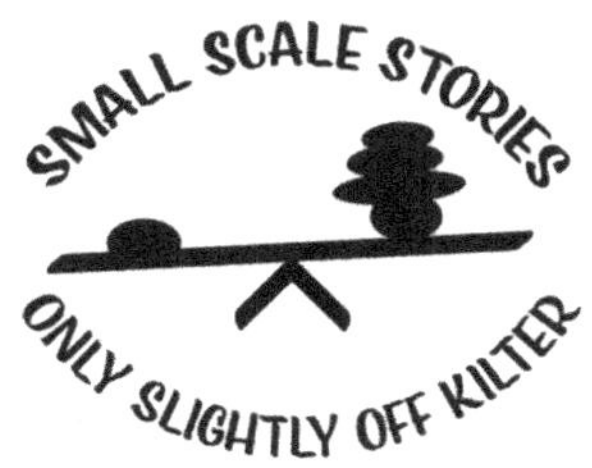

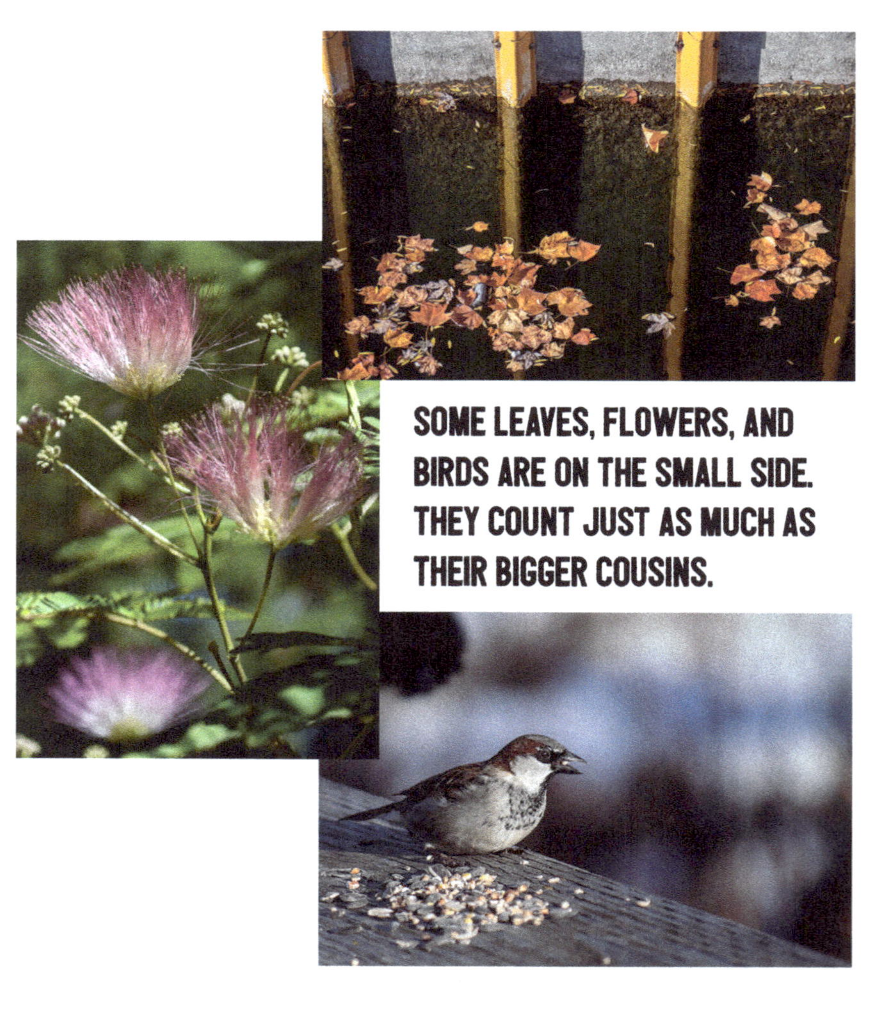

SOME LEAVES, FLOWERS, AND BIRDS ARE ON THE SMALL SIDE. THEY COUNT JUST AS MUCH AS THEIR BIGGER COUSINS.

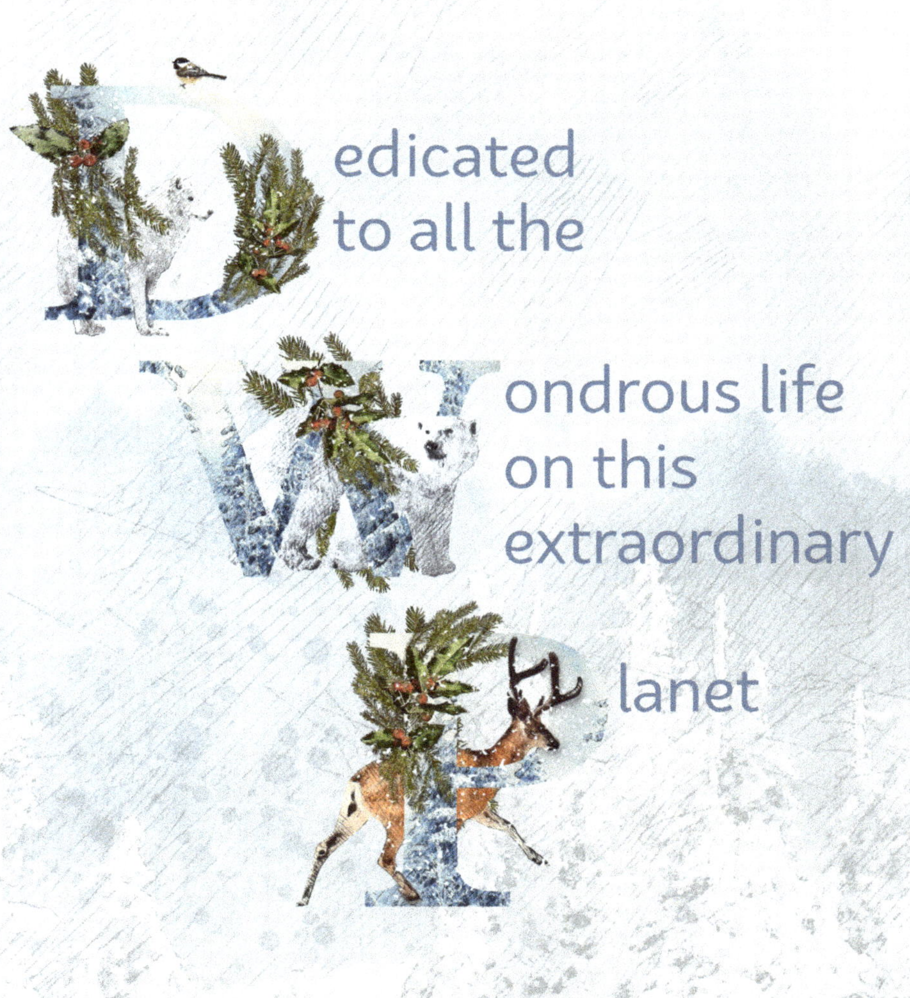

Dedicated to all the Wondrous life on this extraordinary Planet

THE STORIES

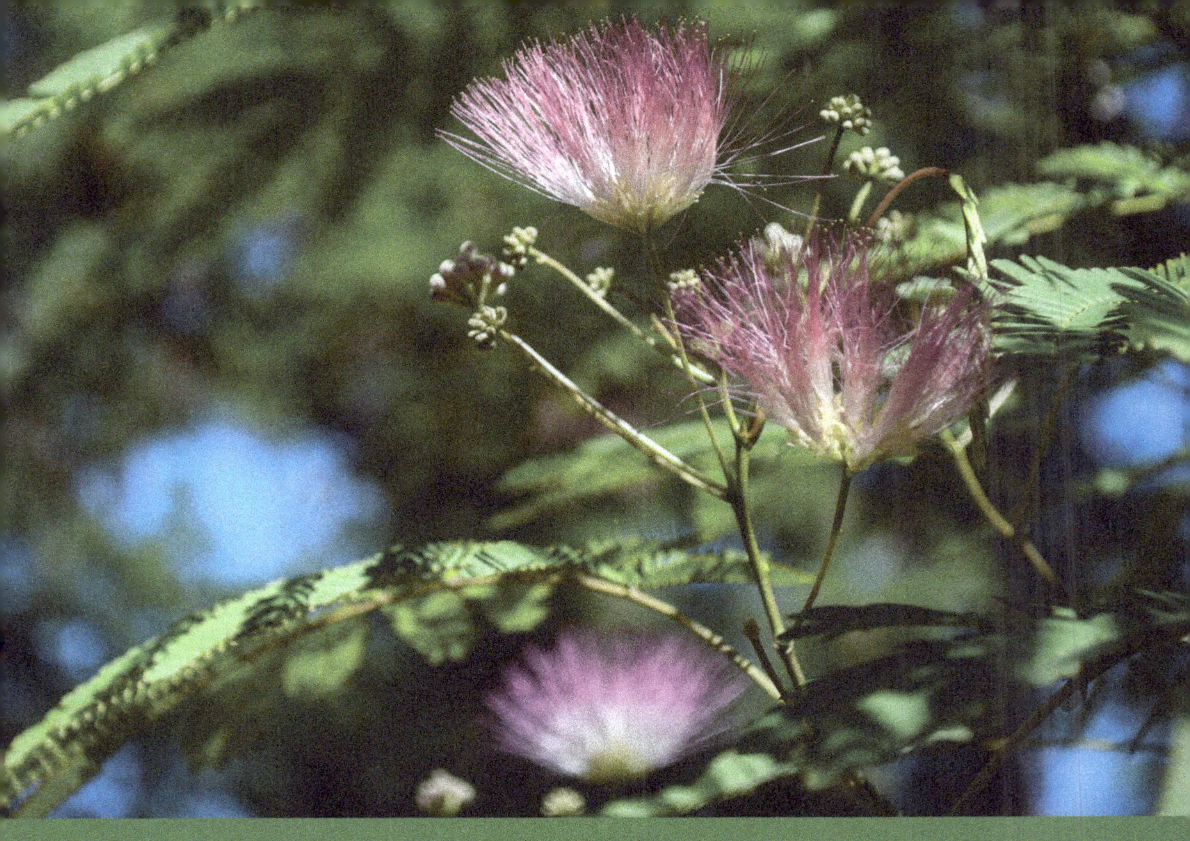

The gardener called her *calliandra surinamensis*. Visitors called her powder puff. The gardener's name was more poetic, but everyone spoke of her with awe. She realized the name was less important than the love behind it.

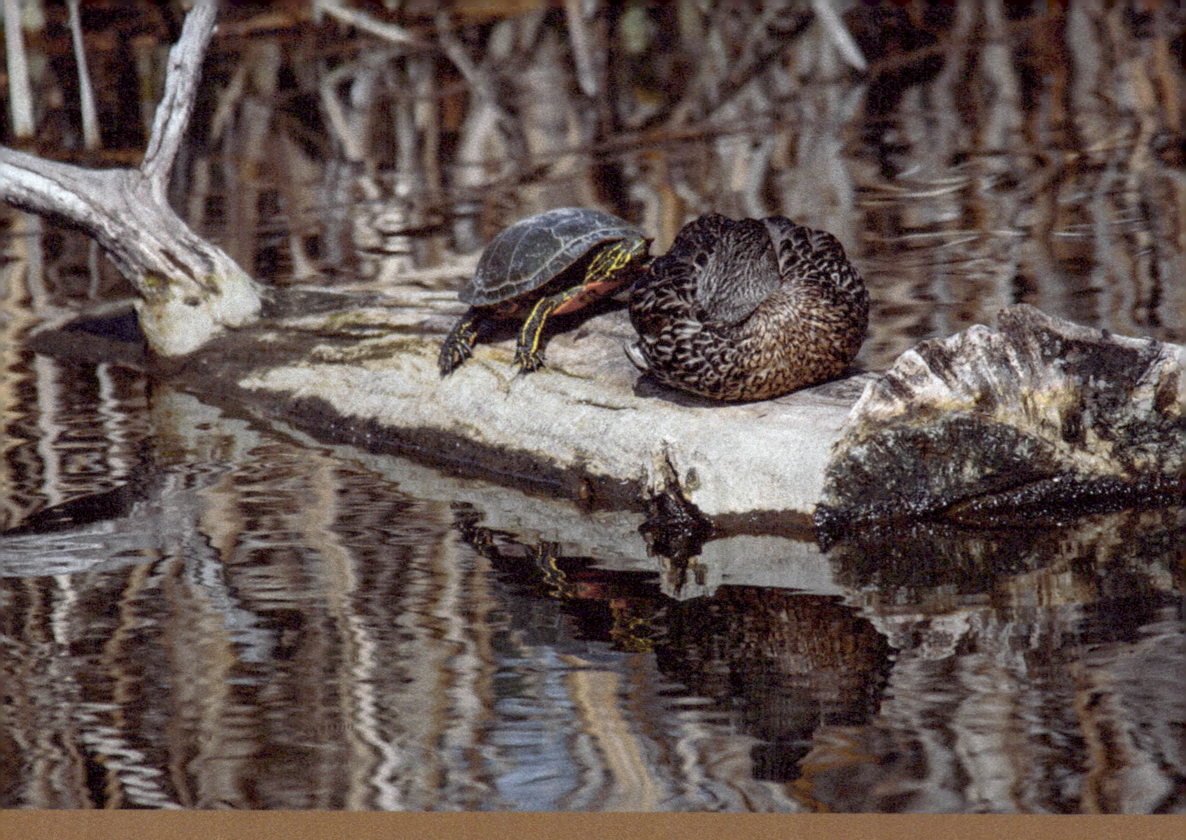

"Hey, Duck, how was your winter? Laid any eggs yet? Still with the same boyfriend? Did it snow much?" Mallard wanted to nap, but she knew Turtle was hungry for marsh news. She sighed and began answering questions.

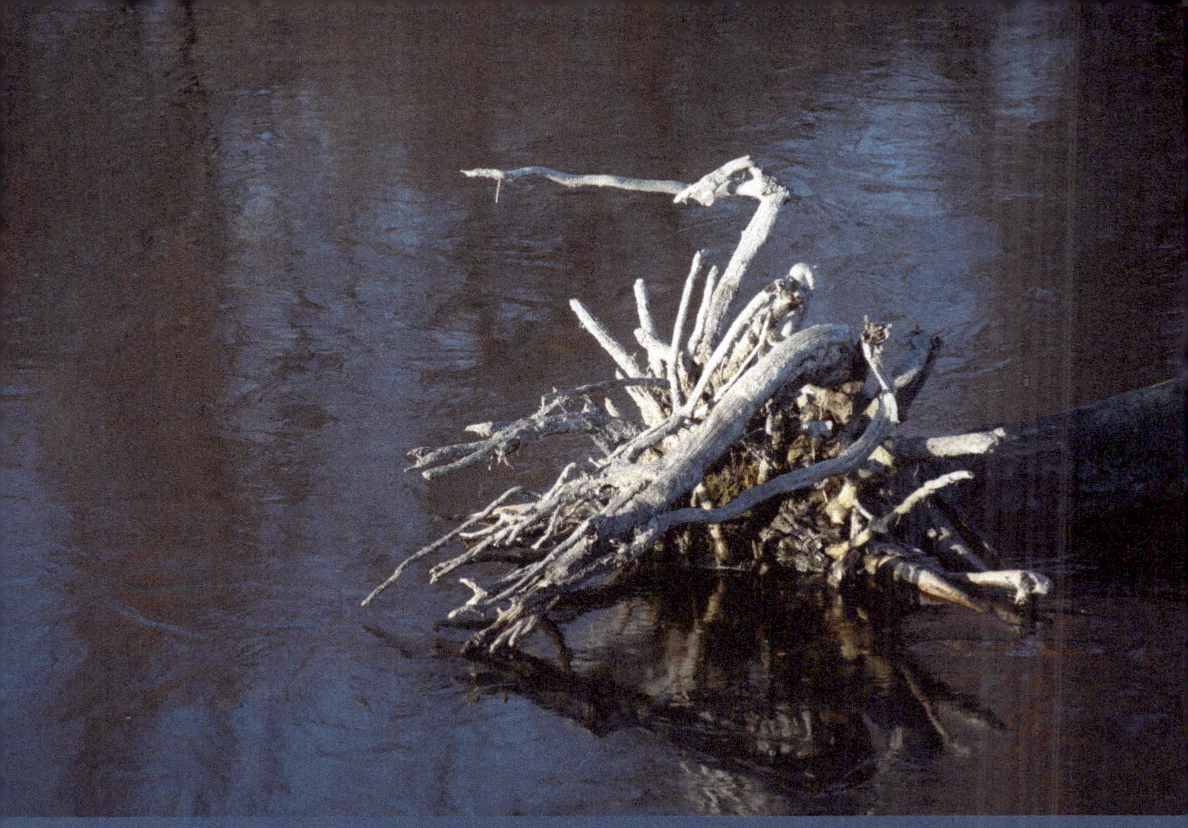

Veronica loved role playing. Some days she was Easy Rider on his Harley. Other days she was Isadora Duncan, before her scarf caught in the wheel. Today she was a headless Baryshnikov, doing a daring pirouette, with leg extended.

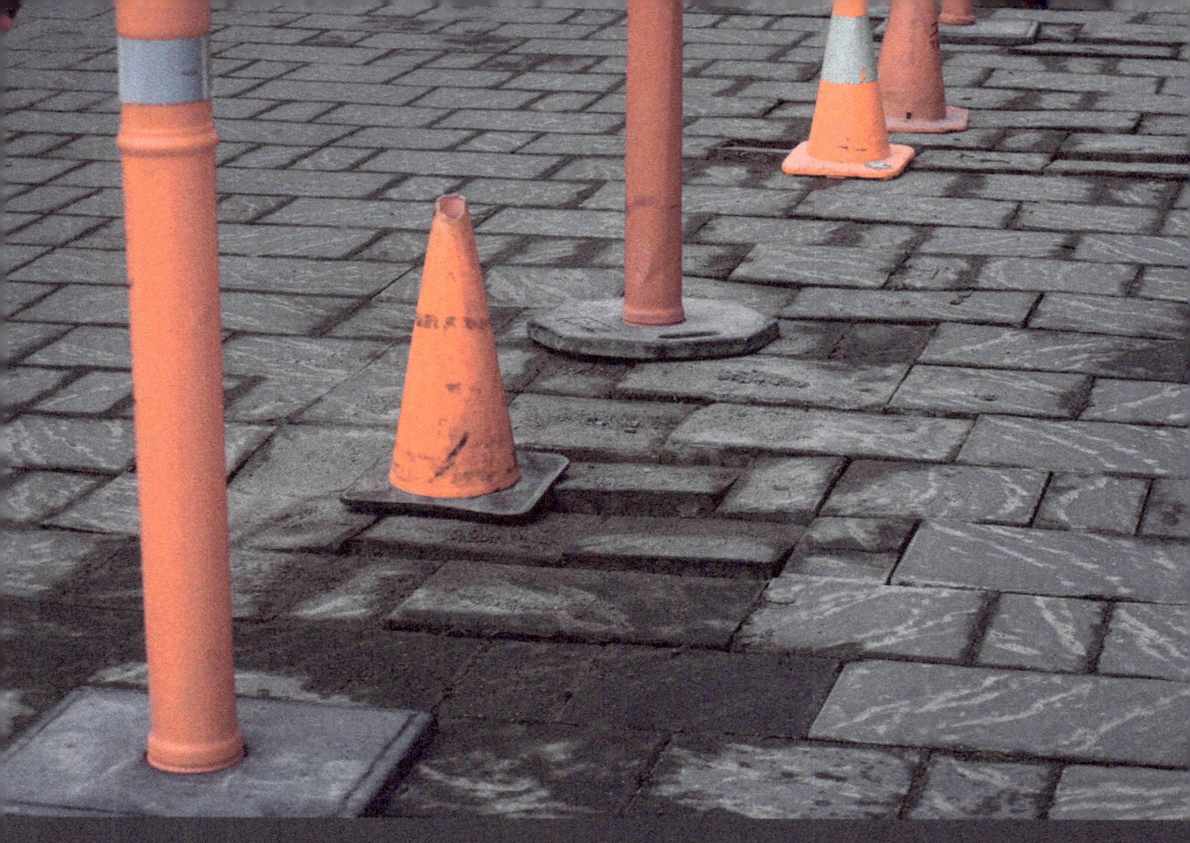

"What happened to you, Shrimp?" Tall Boy looked
down at the bedraggled cone. "Skate boarders,"
sighed Shrimp. "The newbies are pretty hard on me,
but I got my revenge. I tripped a few of them."

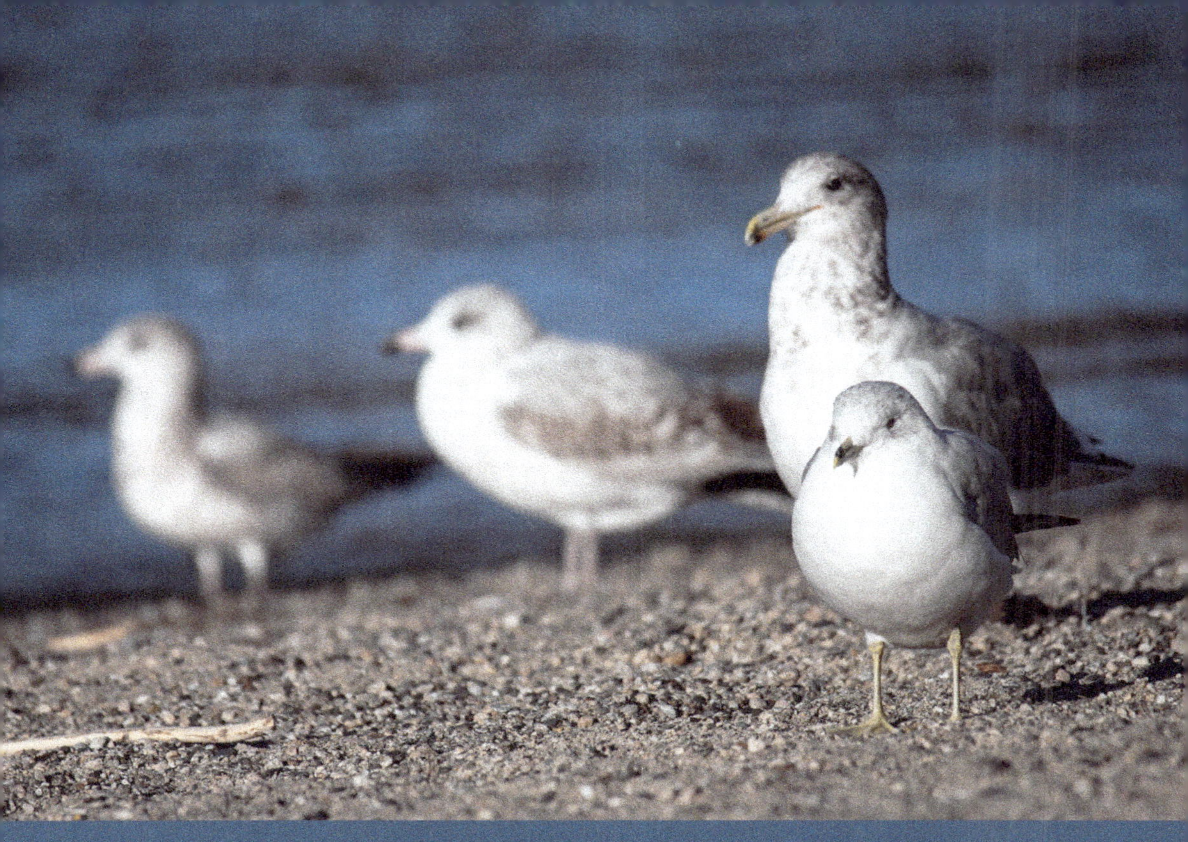

Hazel was on the small side of the young gulls. She tried to make up for it by puffing out her chest. It did not have the desired effect. "Are you cold?" asked Gabby. Hazel sighed. She would have to try something else.

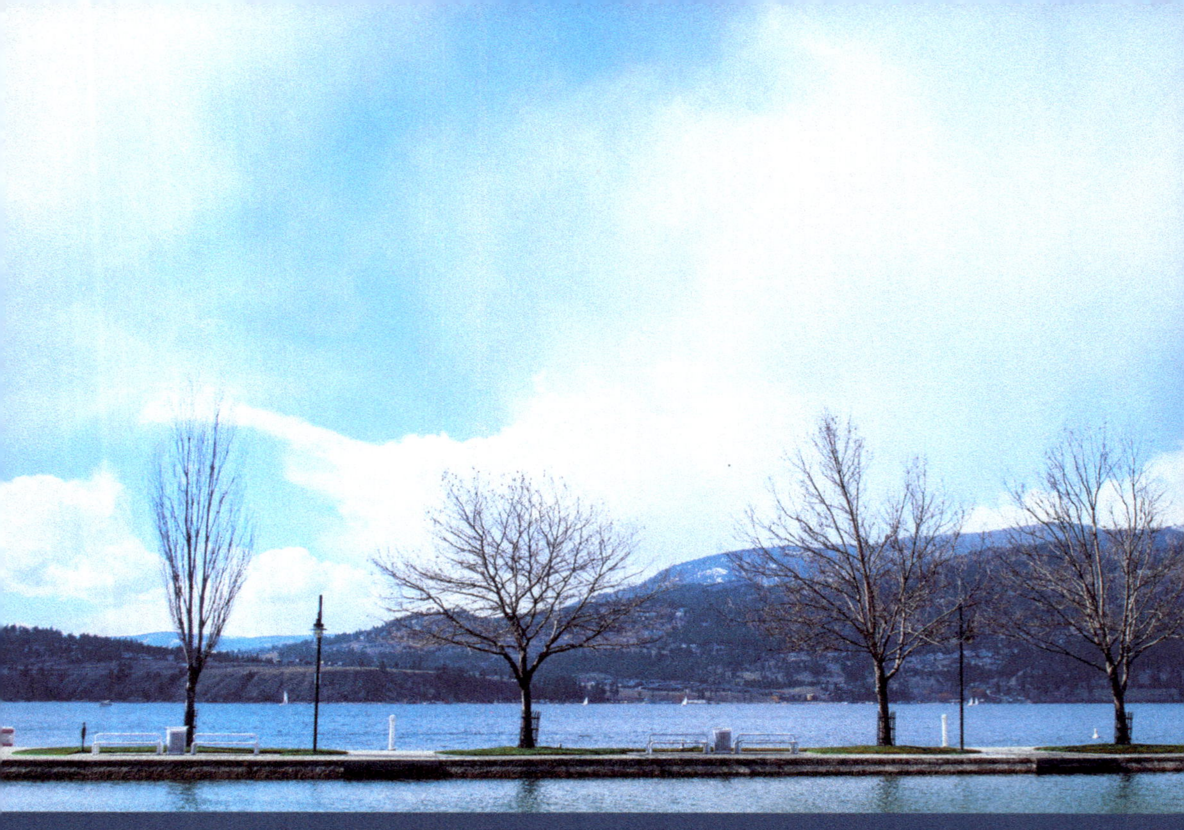

The three tree sisters sent messages to Slim, sometimes through wind or birds, other times through the thin threads of mushrooms. They liked their different neighbor and wanted to be sure he knew he was appreciated.

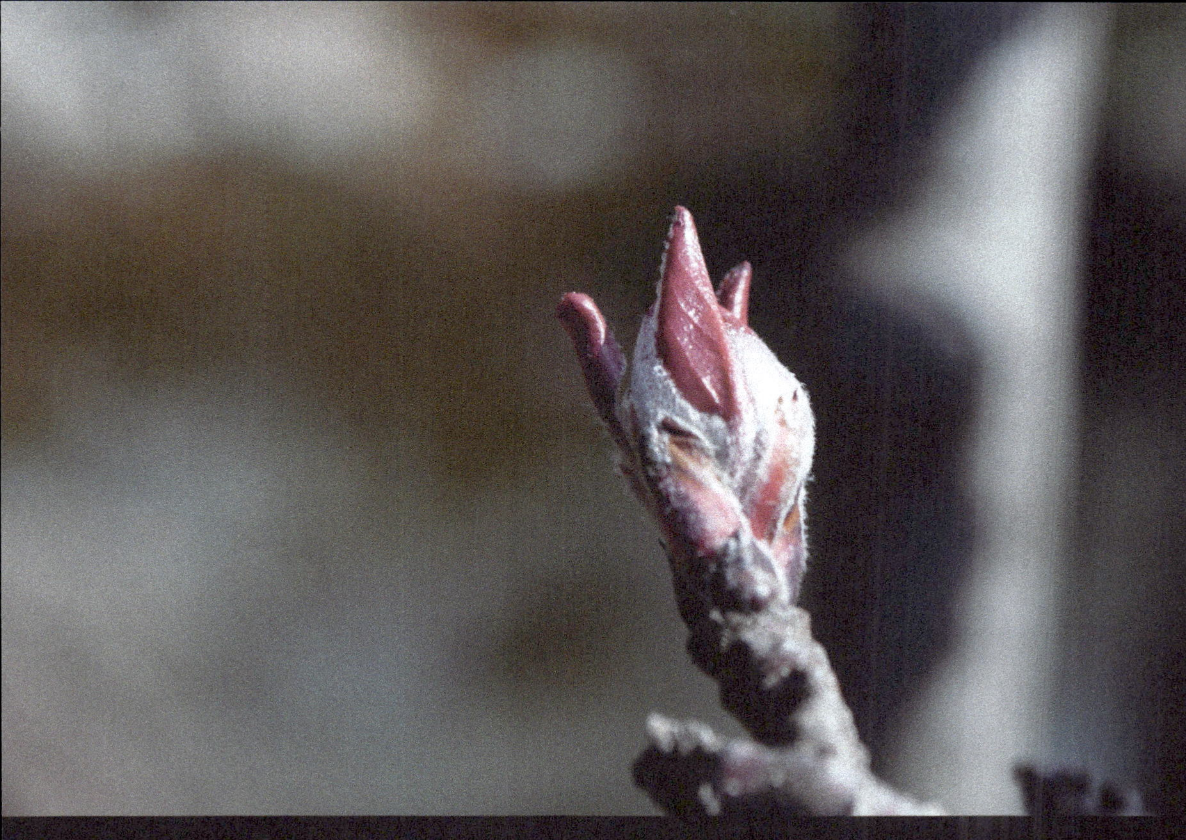

She felt shy and uncertain as she slowly unfolded.
On cool, grey days, she longed to curl back into a
bud. But Life was insistent. She had no choice but to
move forward.

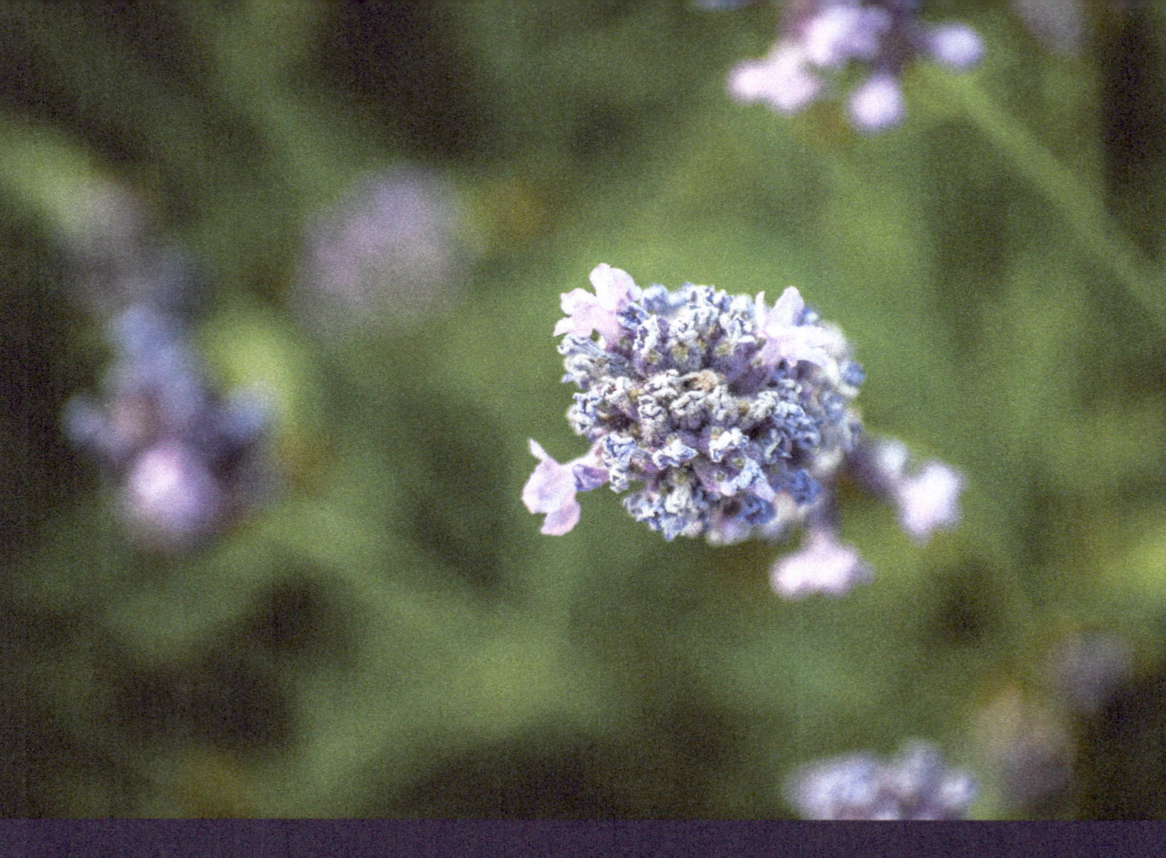

"Lonely, I am so lonely..." Lavender sang plaintively. The other lavender flower heads laughed. "You couldn't be lonely even if you wanted to," they said, "not with all of us nearby". Lavender sighed and thought how little they understood introverts.

"You're on the chunky side," said Post Shadow. He had been quiet all summer, overwhelmed by all swirling shadows of children and grownups and birds. Now he was ready for some friendly chat, but he had forgotten how to make polite conversation.

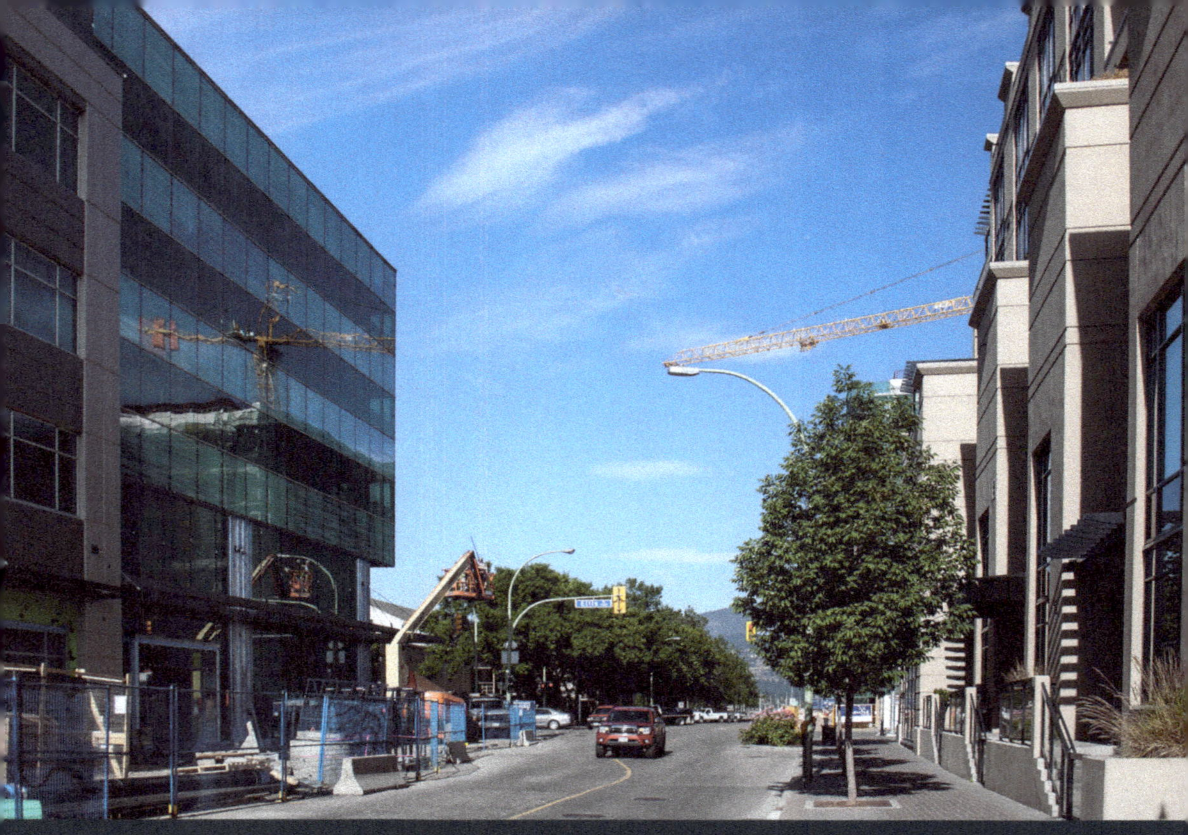

Crane swung around and caught sight of his reflection in the new building. He had never seen his image before. For the rest of the day, the crane operator found him surprisingly recalcitrant, unwilling to swing to another angle.

Spider looked in satisfaction at the fruits of her weaving. She had had a splendid day. The flies were less thrilled.

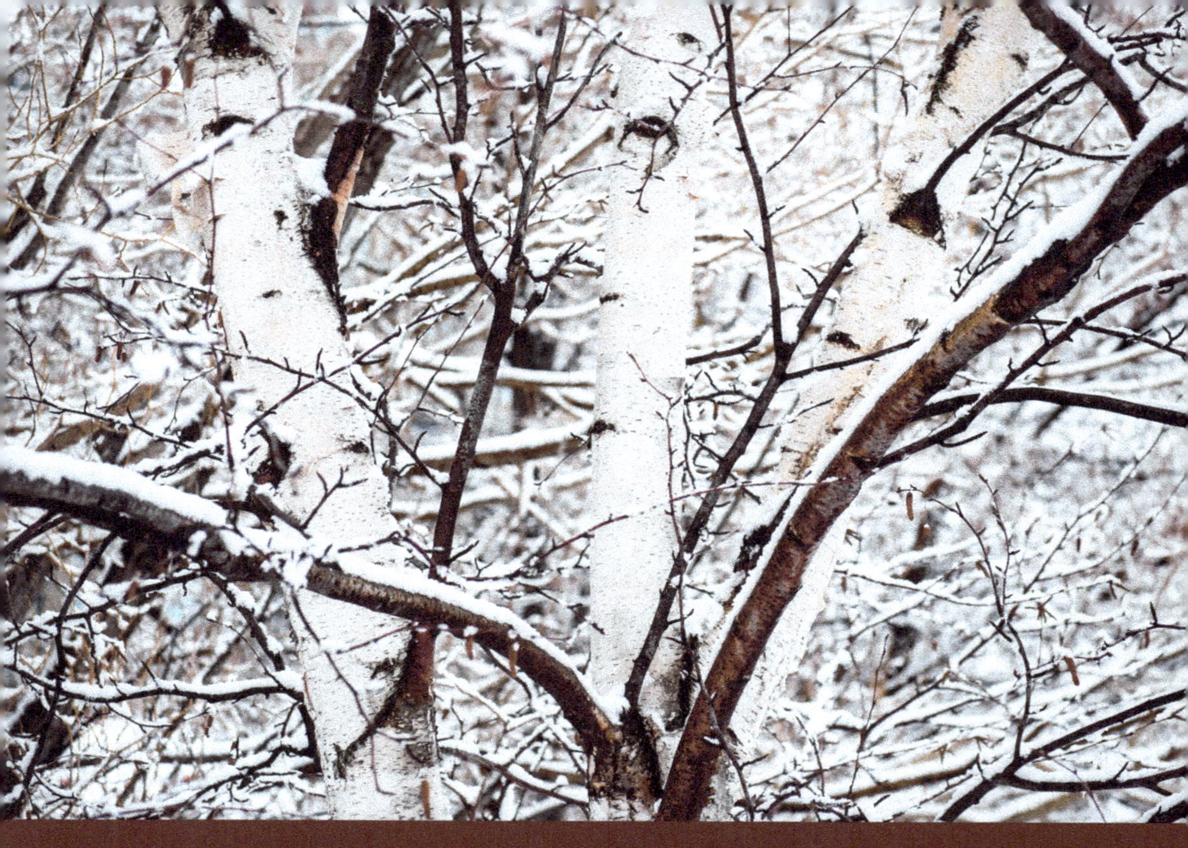

The triplets loved winter best of all. Once their summer leaves fell, nothing hid their slender figures. Snowy days were their favorite, showing off their graceful limbs.

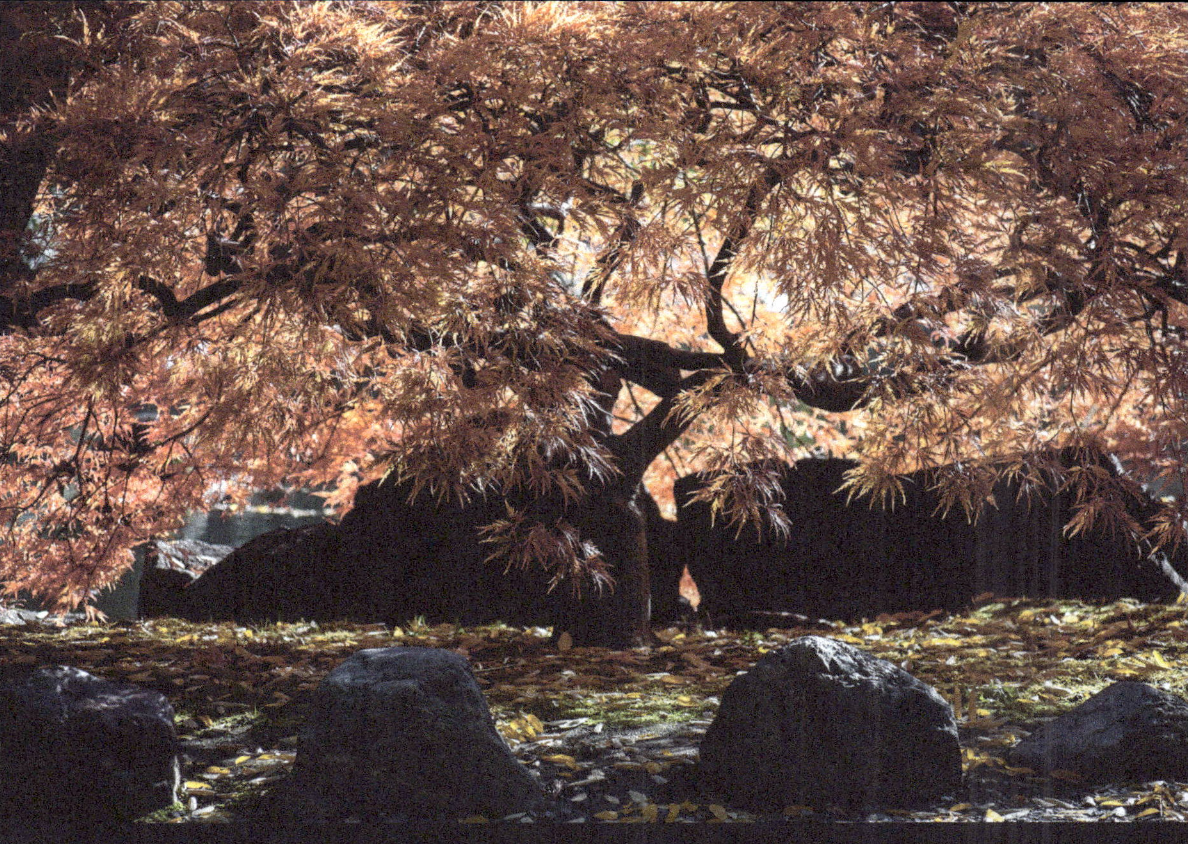

The Faery Ball had been a big success. Japanese Maple knew they usually chose a different site for it each year, but she hoped next year they would remember that everyone agreed her decorations were the best they had ever seen.

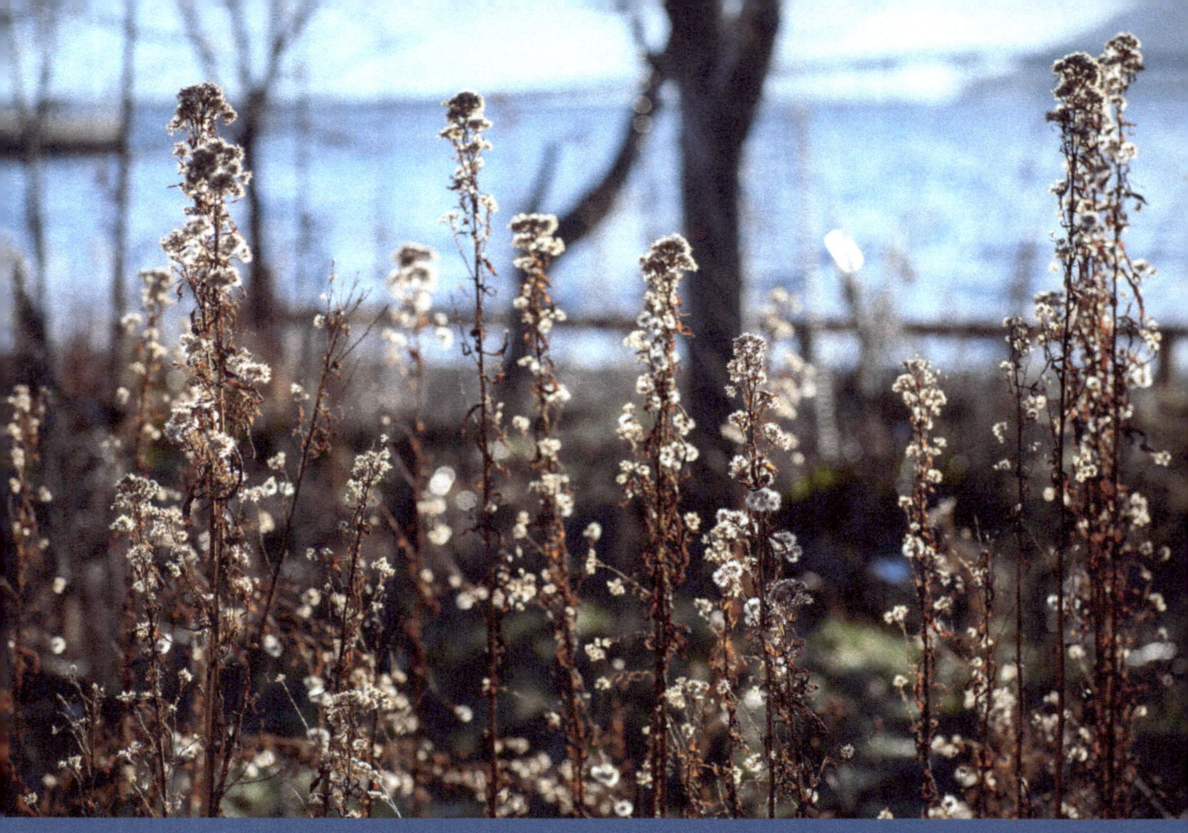

Their blooms long turned to seed, their slender stems dry with age, they no longer felt beautiful. Sun understood and gilded them from top to bottom. Their radiance caught the eyes of passersby, who stopped to admire them.

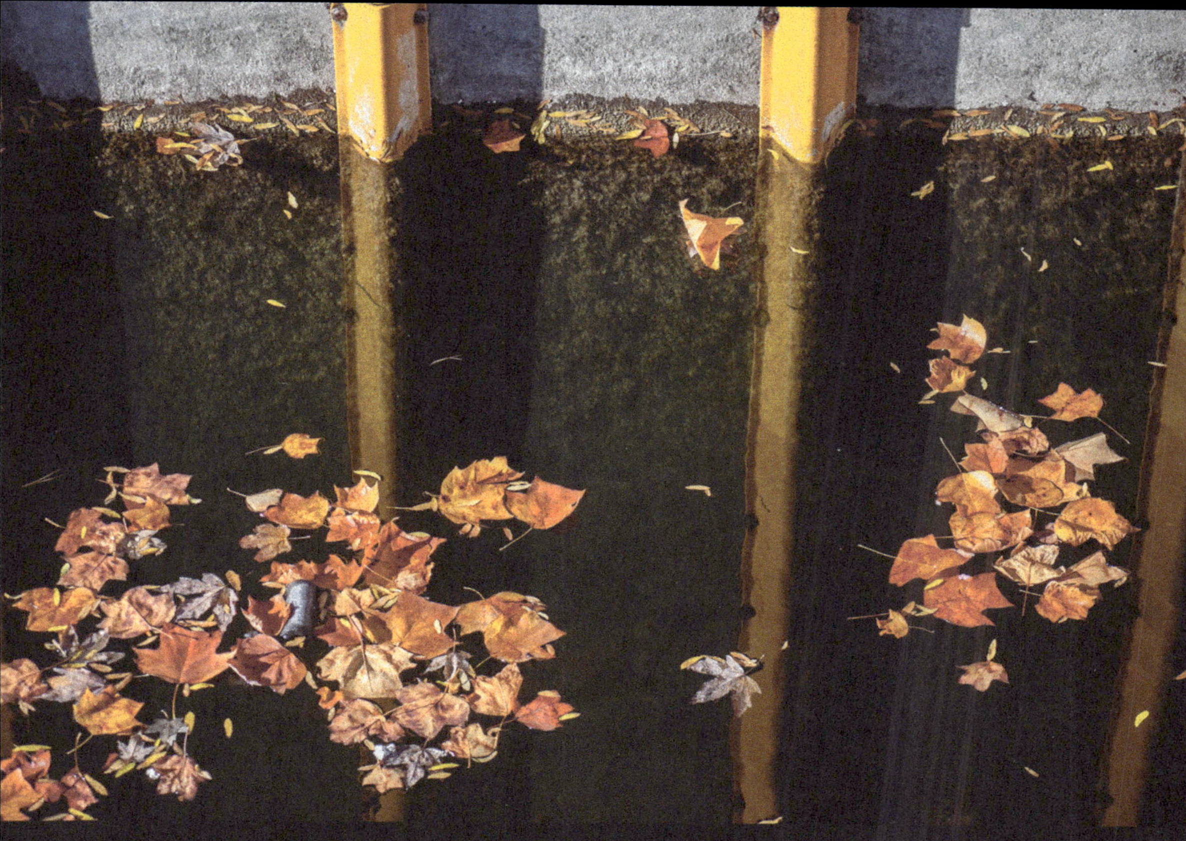

All summer the leaves had wondered what was in
the locks. After falling, they could see how much
they brightened the rather drab cement walls and
how happy the yellow poles were to meet them.

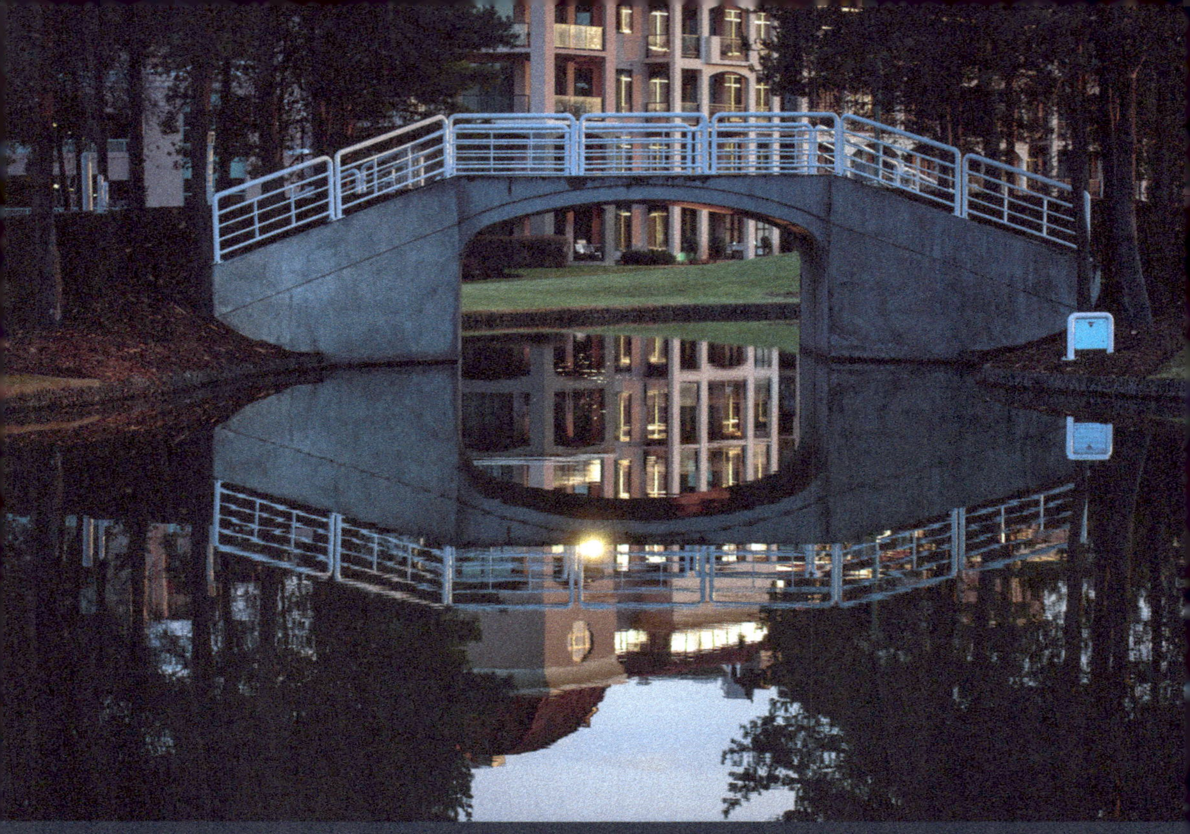

On still evenings, Bridge and Water loved to play opera singer. People crossing the bridge were mostly clueless, but once in a while a finely tuned mind caught notes from a mysterious voice. A few even thought they recognized an aria.

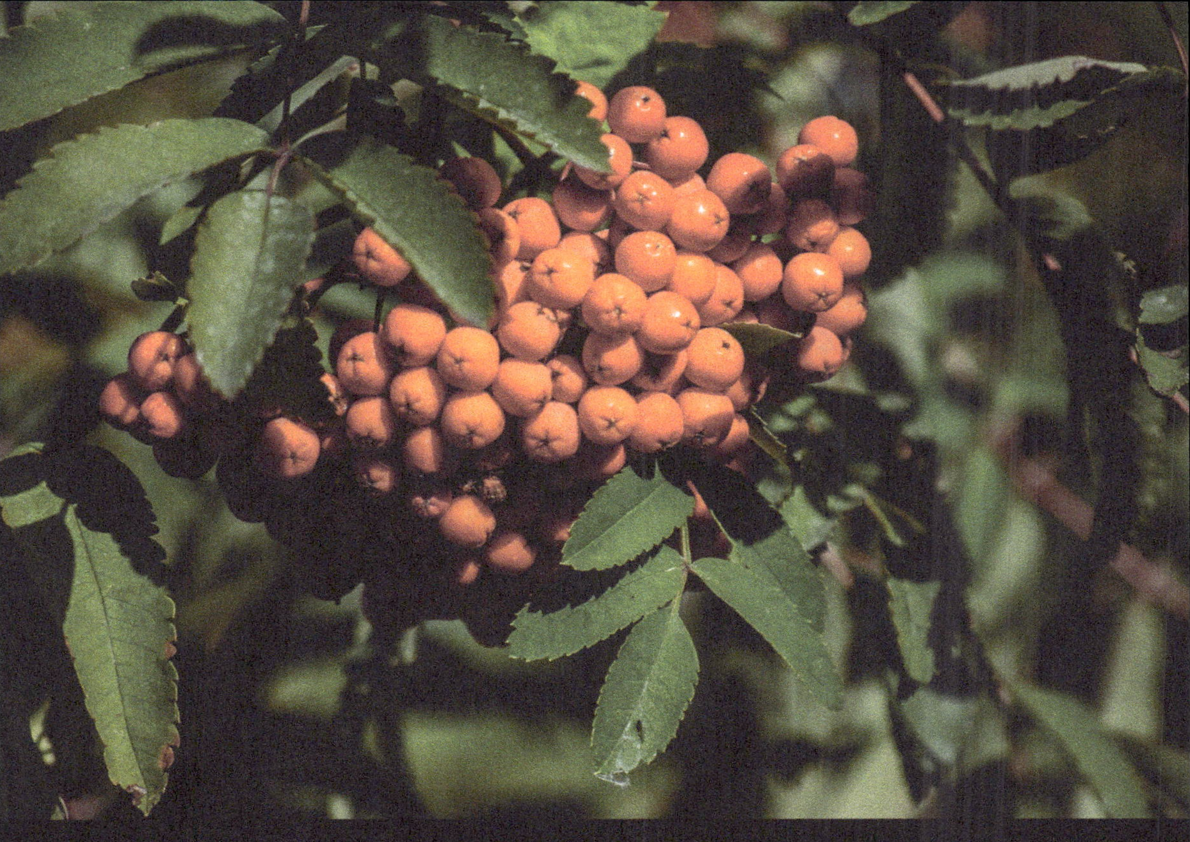

Berries began as white flowers, then morphed into clusters of orange berries. They had listened to their parent trees whisper about magpies and knew what was ahead. They would lose their lovely outer coatings, but their seeds would start new trees.

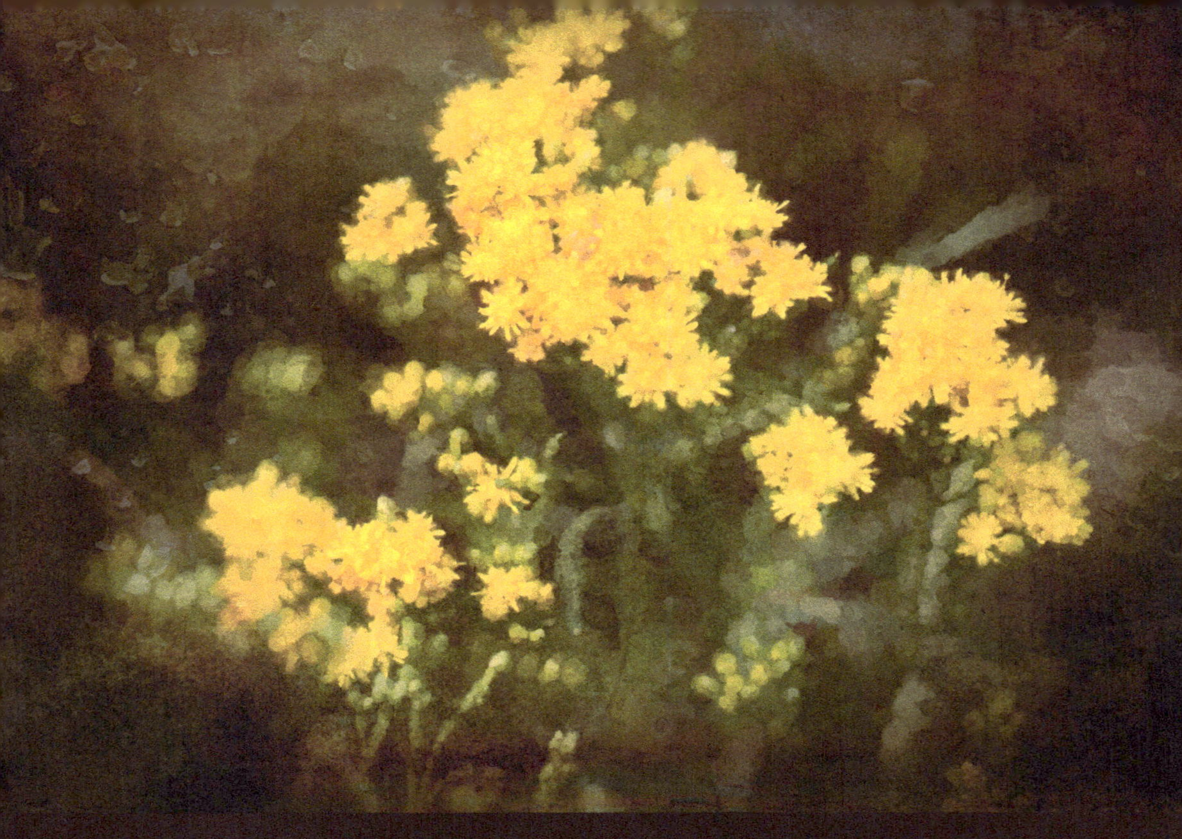

"I feel old," said the cluster of yellow flowers. The nearby stones chuckled. "You don't know what old is, but if that photographer lady ever shows you what she did with that last photo of you, you'll croak right on the spot."

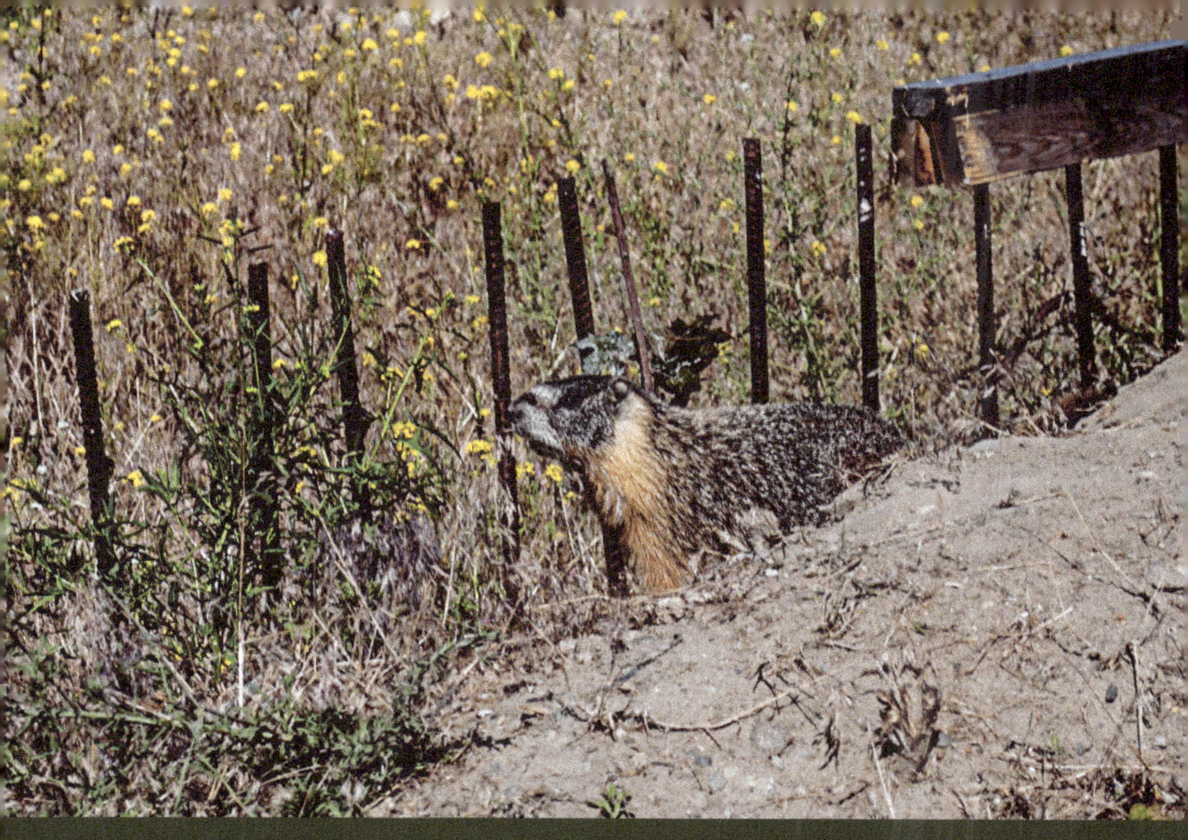

"The diggers are coming! The diggers are coming!" The old marmots scurried for the tunnels. Artis was too young to know what diggers were. He stayed outside long enough to see his mountain torn down, then ran for safety.

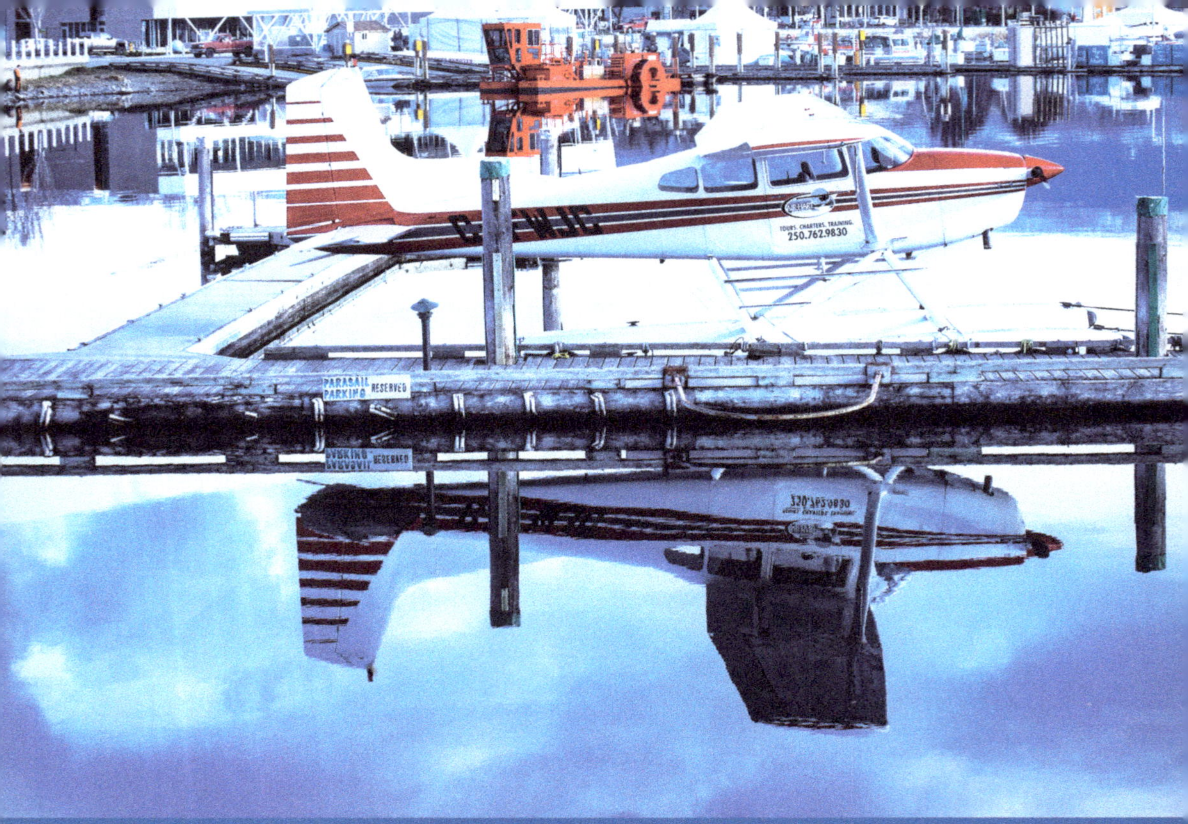

Plane missed his waterfront friends during the long winter. Back at his berth, he waited for Wind to tip his wings in greeting to docks, boats and water. When Wind was still, he admired his own reflection. Soon he would be aloft. He sighed with satisfaction.

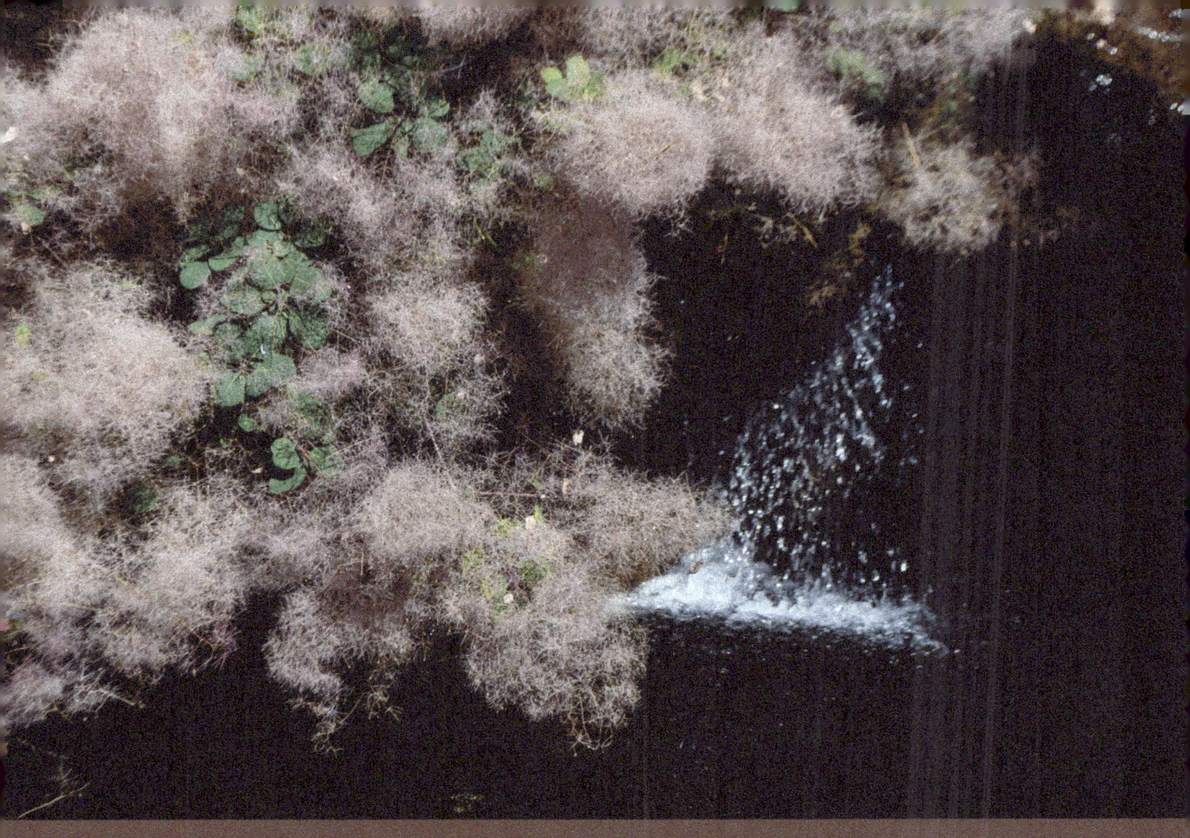

Smoke bush laughed. Falls Water had not run over the stones all winter. Pool Water had been silent. Suddenly stones and pond were swirling with crazy stories, stored up during the quiet of winter. Smoke bush loved to listen.

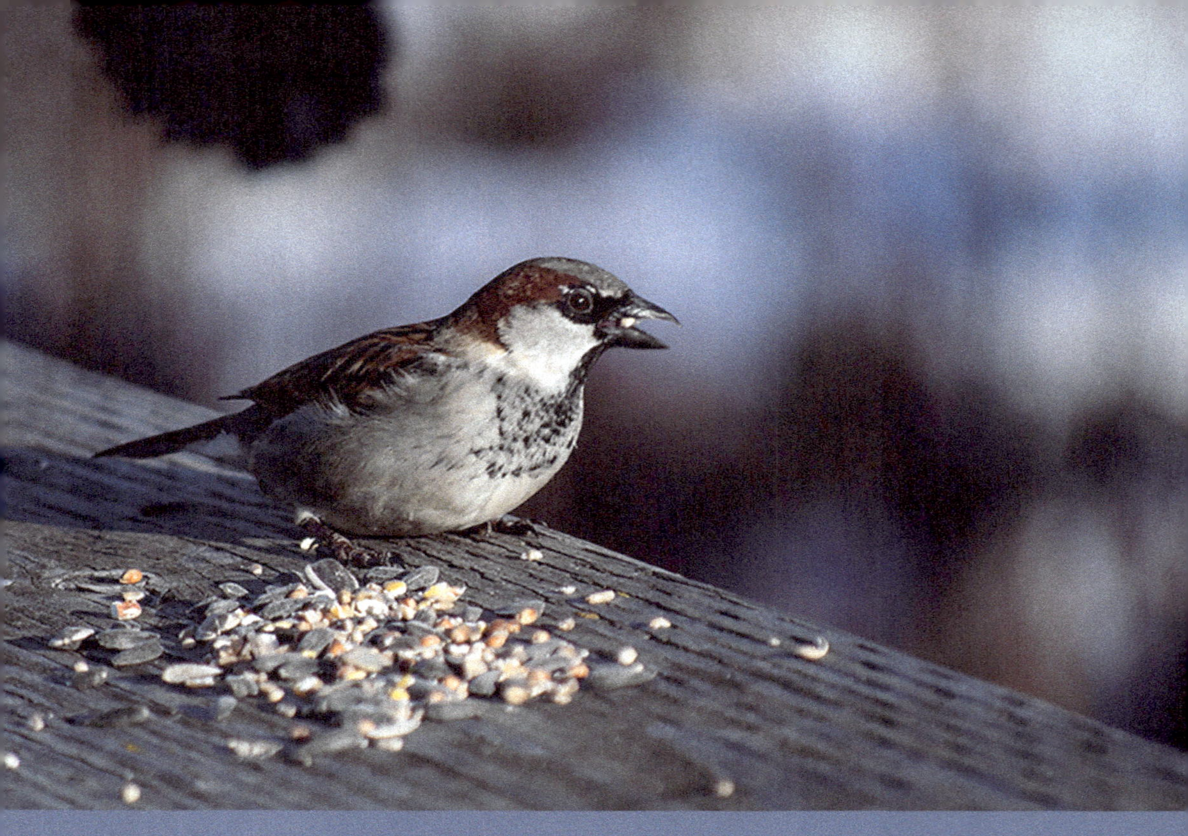

"Listen, Red-Winged Blackbird, you are a coward."
When the human came near, you flew. I see your tail.
Watch me walk right up to them. You think sparrows
are small and weak. We are small and MIGHTY."

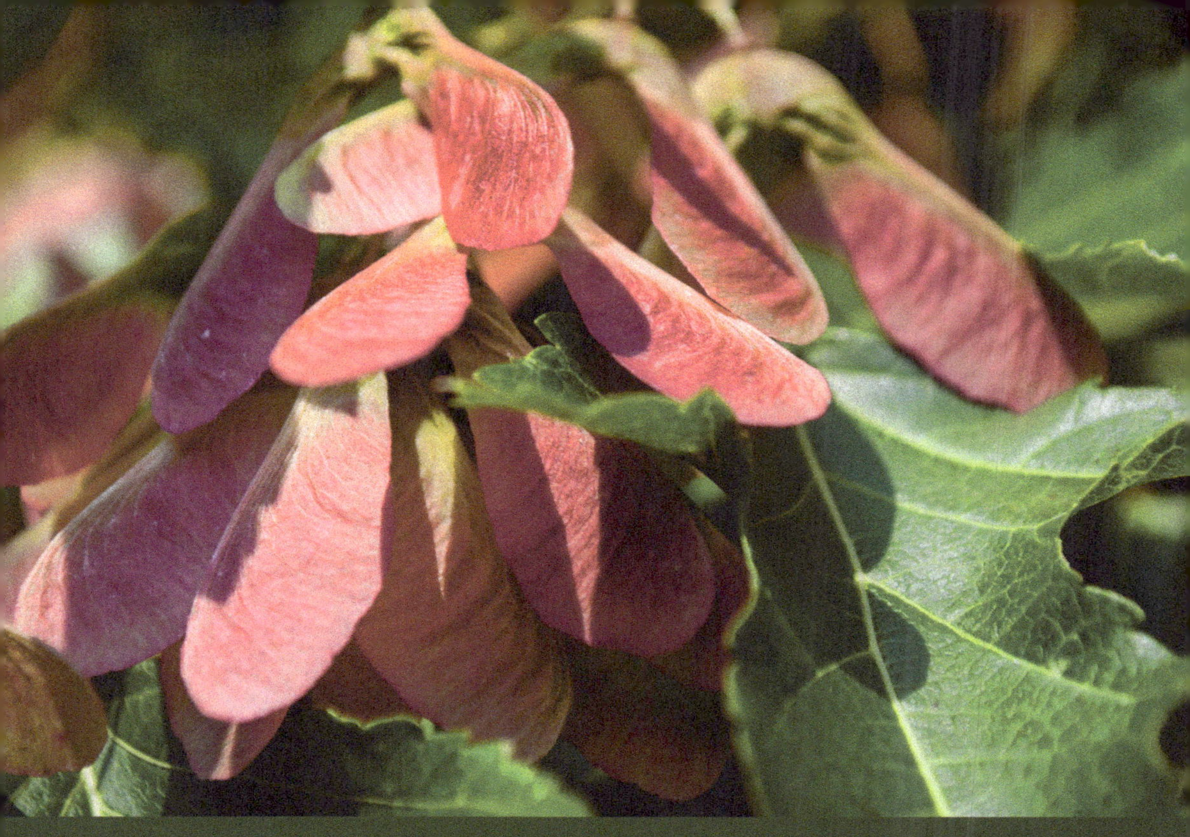

"It's a beautiful day…ay…ay…ay…It's a beautiful day!" sang Top Seed Pod. The others were fretting, as their lovely green hues turned to red. Top Seed Pod's song made them happy to be alive and changing.

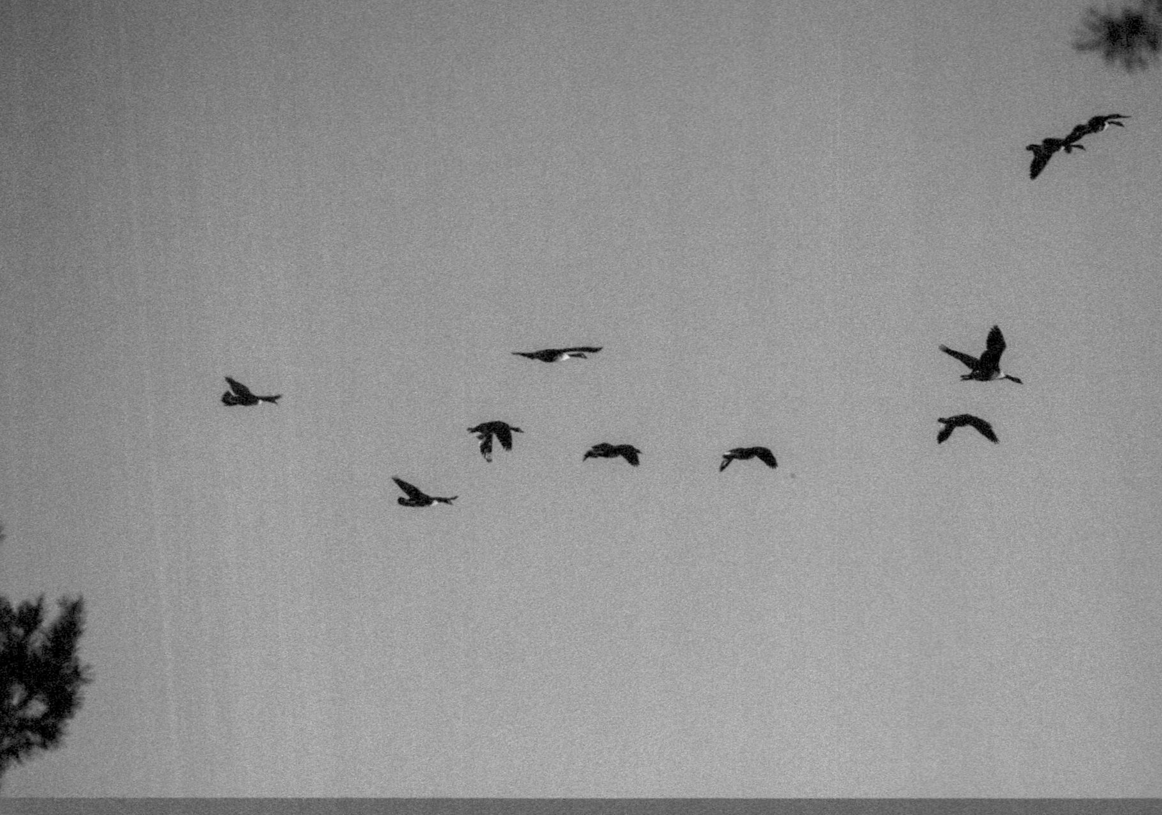

As they moved into landing position, they hoped no one was watching. This late in the day, their formations were always a bit ragged.

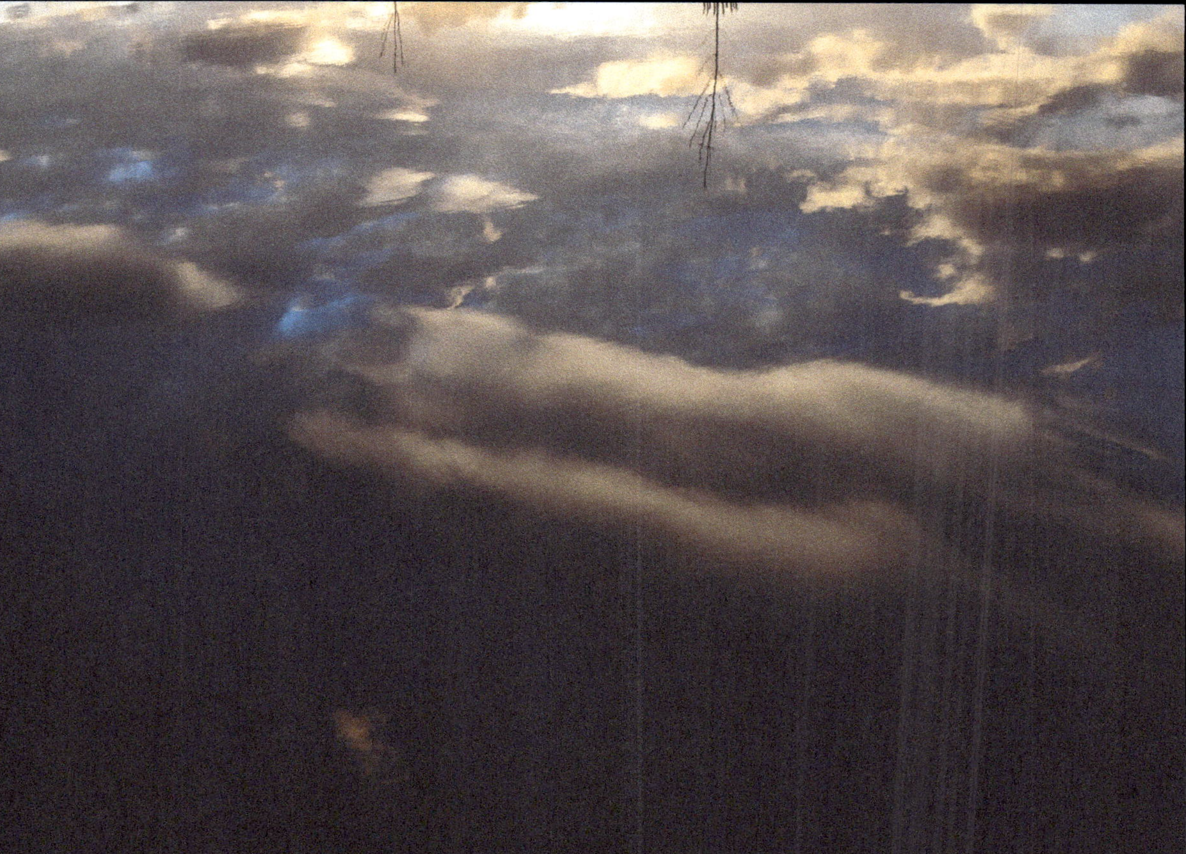

The two little trees stared down at their reflections in the lagoon. The smallest said, "Do you think we'll ever be big enough to touch the clouds?" Wanting to reassure his sibling, older brother said confidently, "Soon. Yes, very soon."

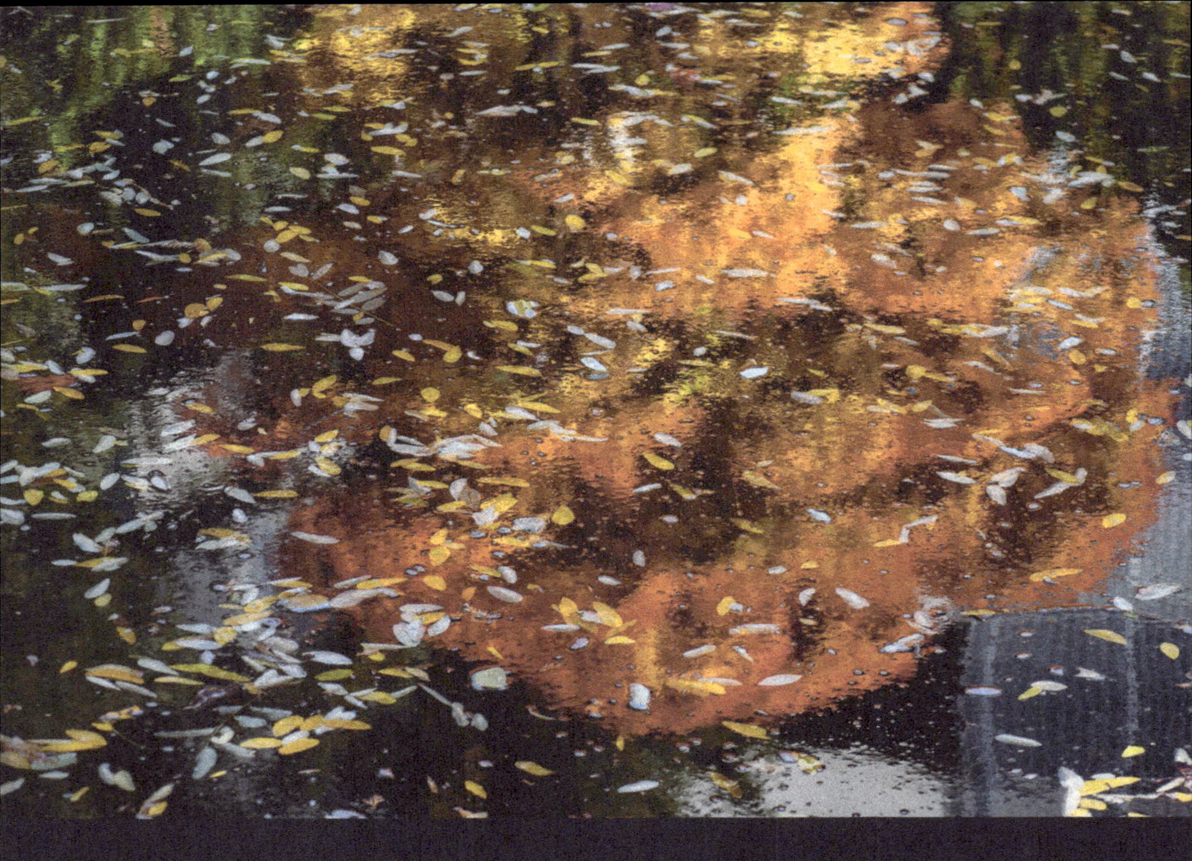

The fallen leaves gathered in the water, waiting in hushed expectation. Leaves had been practicing for the Autumn Symphony. They knew it would be their best music ever.

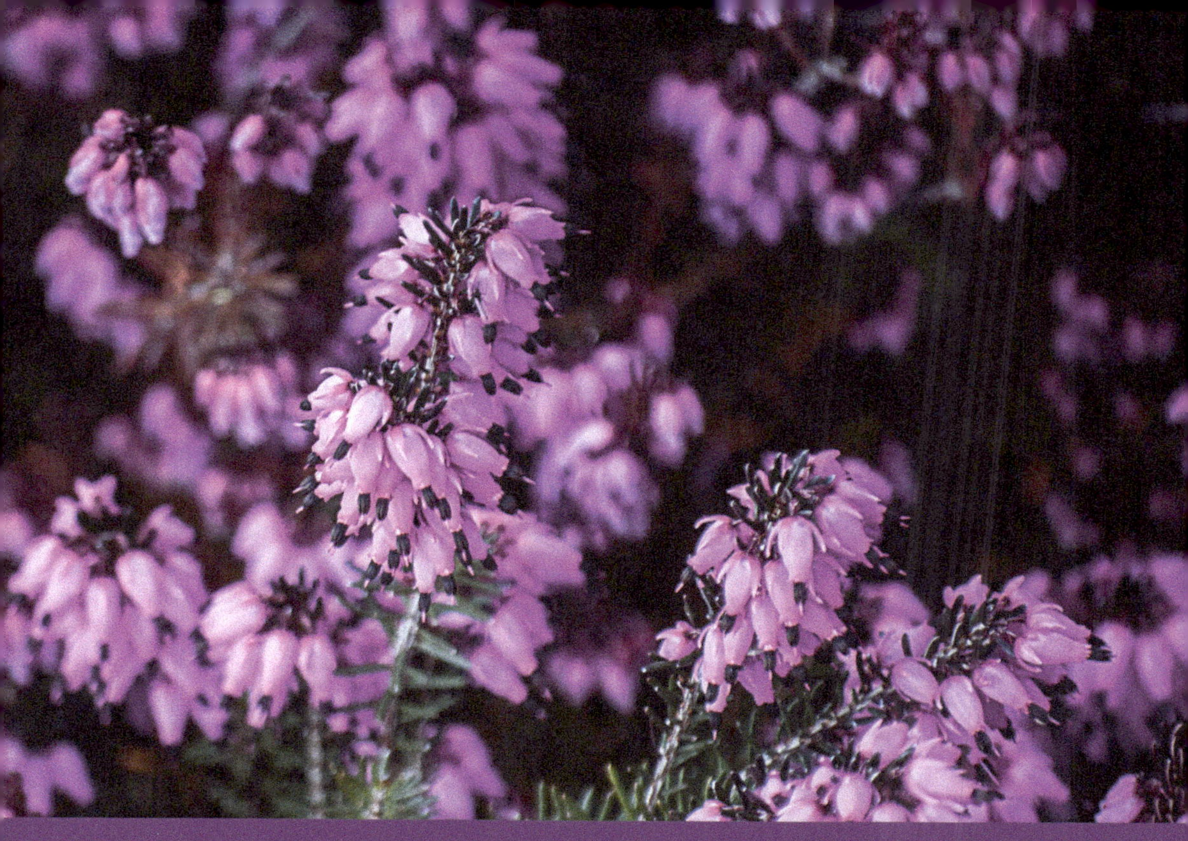

Heather loved being one of the first to bloom in spring. Her ancestors had dotted hillsides in faraway places, but she was a city flower. She had no nearby relatives to natter on about the good old days, when sheep grazed on them in winter.

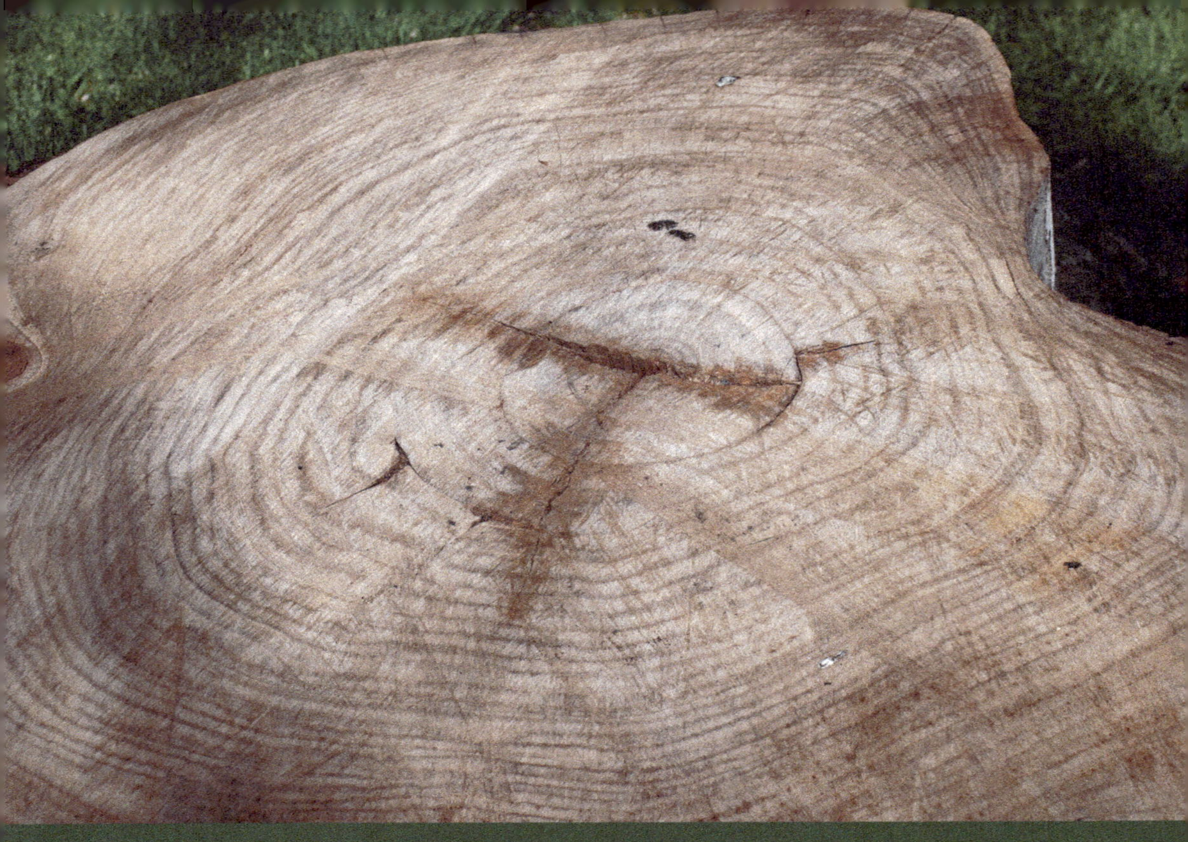

Stump missed his tree. He had lost his sense of meaning and wondered what the City Loggers would do to him, now that they had cut him so low.

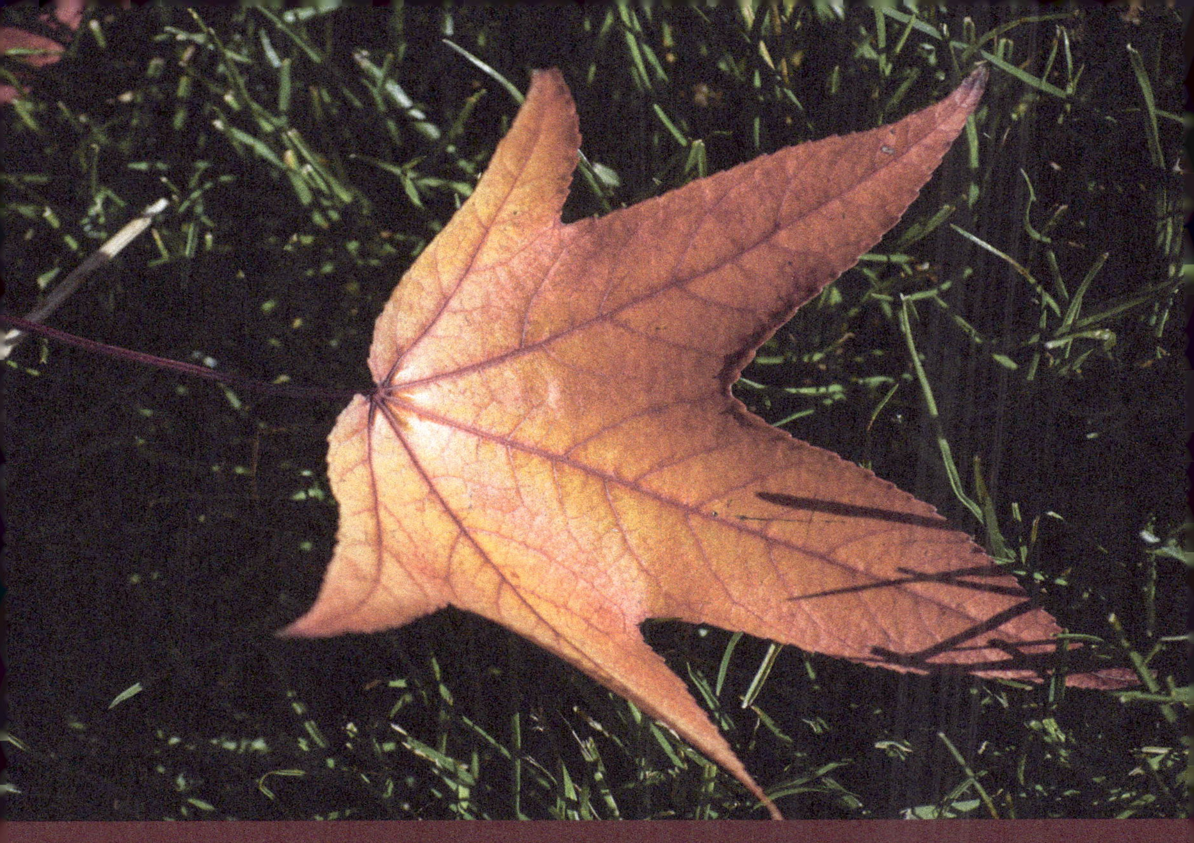

Grass was only a temporary stop for Leaf. She was destined for better things and was only waiting for Wind to whirl her skyward and send her off on her next adventure. She had a list of places she had heard people rave about as she clung to her tree.

He winked at
the woman
who stopped
to study his
wrinkled face.
Her reaction
was not the
terrified
scream he
wanted. She
laughed and
pointed a
camera at
him. So now
he was a joke?
Wait until
Halloween!

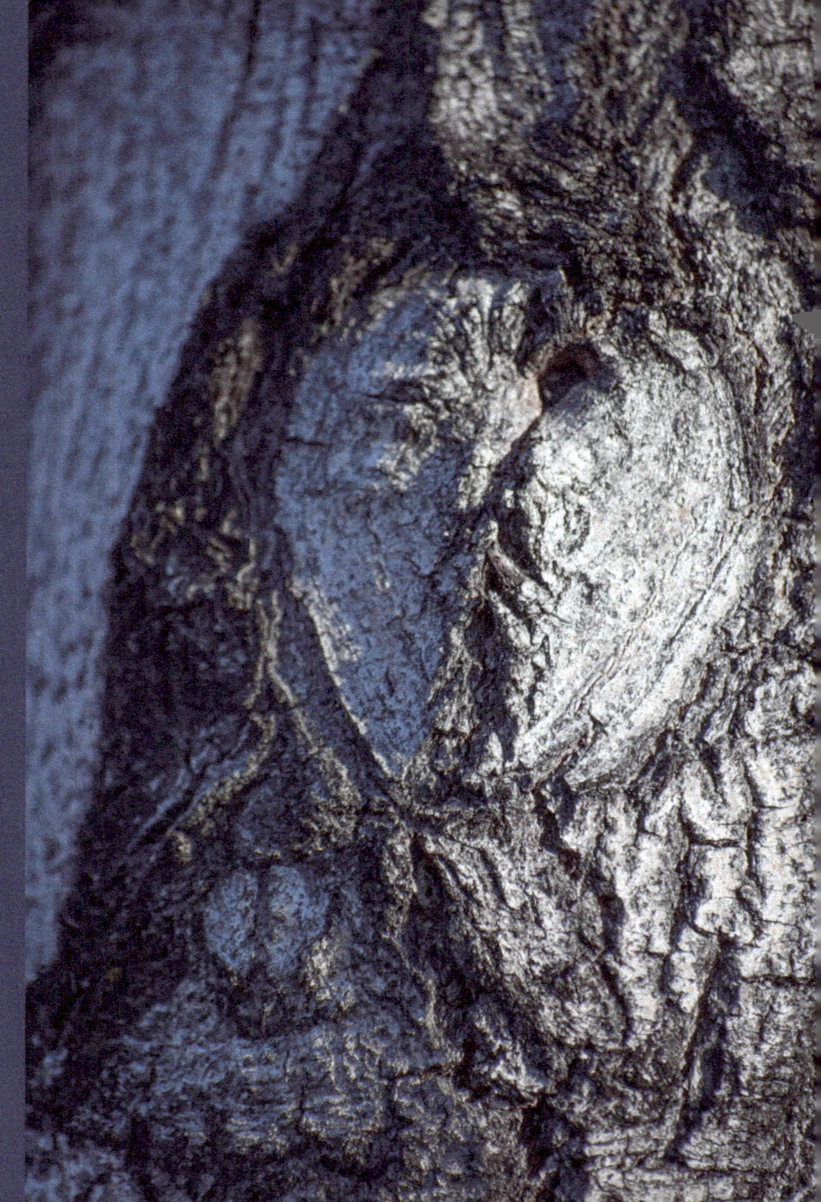

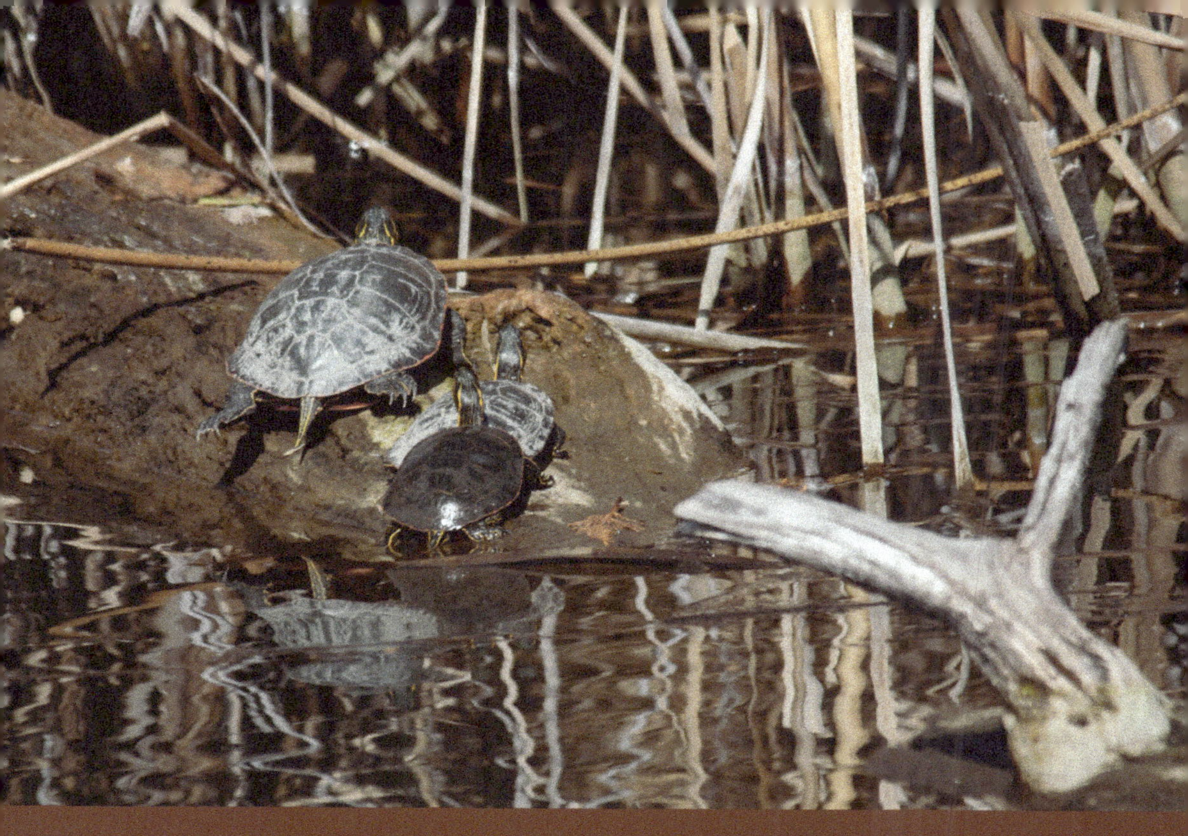

"Move, everybody. I want some of that sunshine too."
Grandmother Turtle sighed. Youngsters were so
impatient these days.

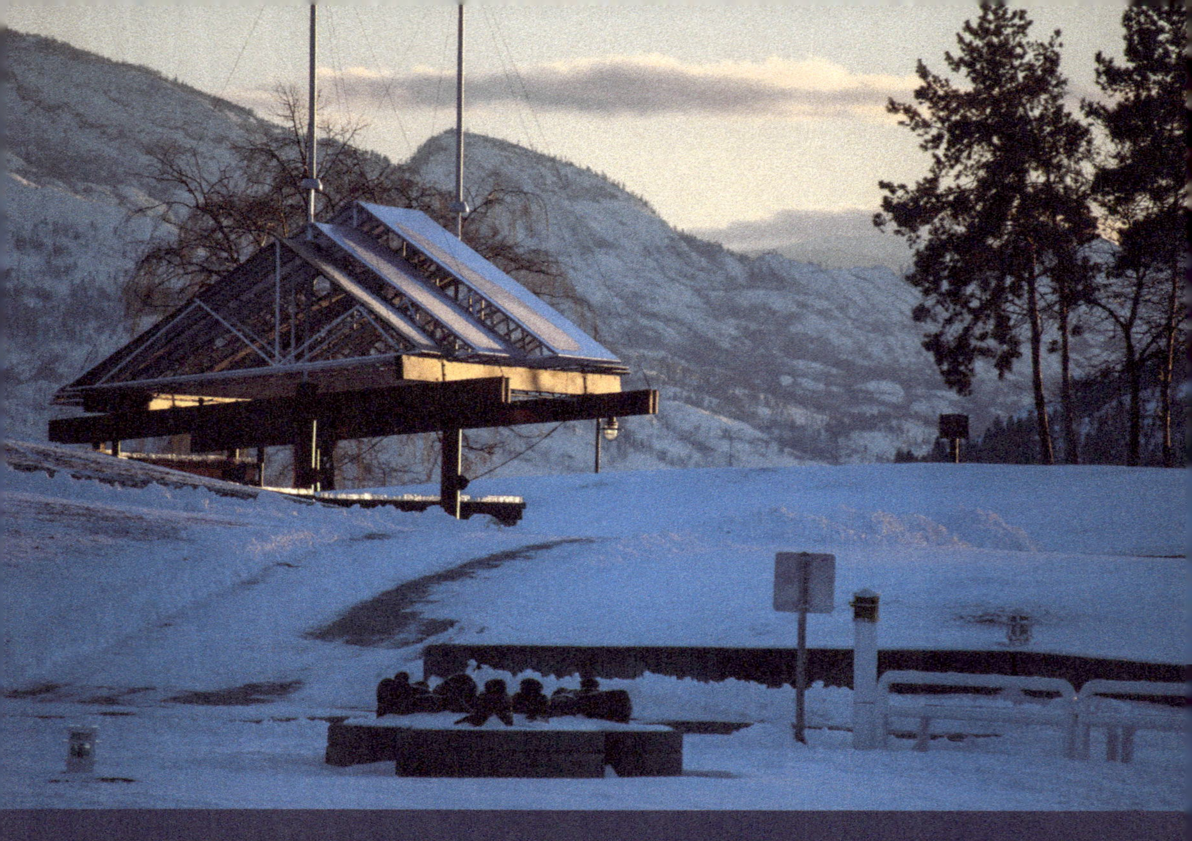

All summer Stage absorbed the sounds of bands and speakers and dancers. When winter came, he whispered the stories and hummed the songs to trees, snow, and hills. They seldom applauded, but he knew they appreciated the entertainment.

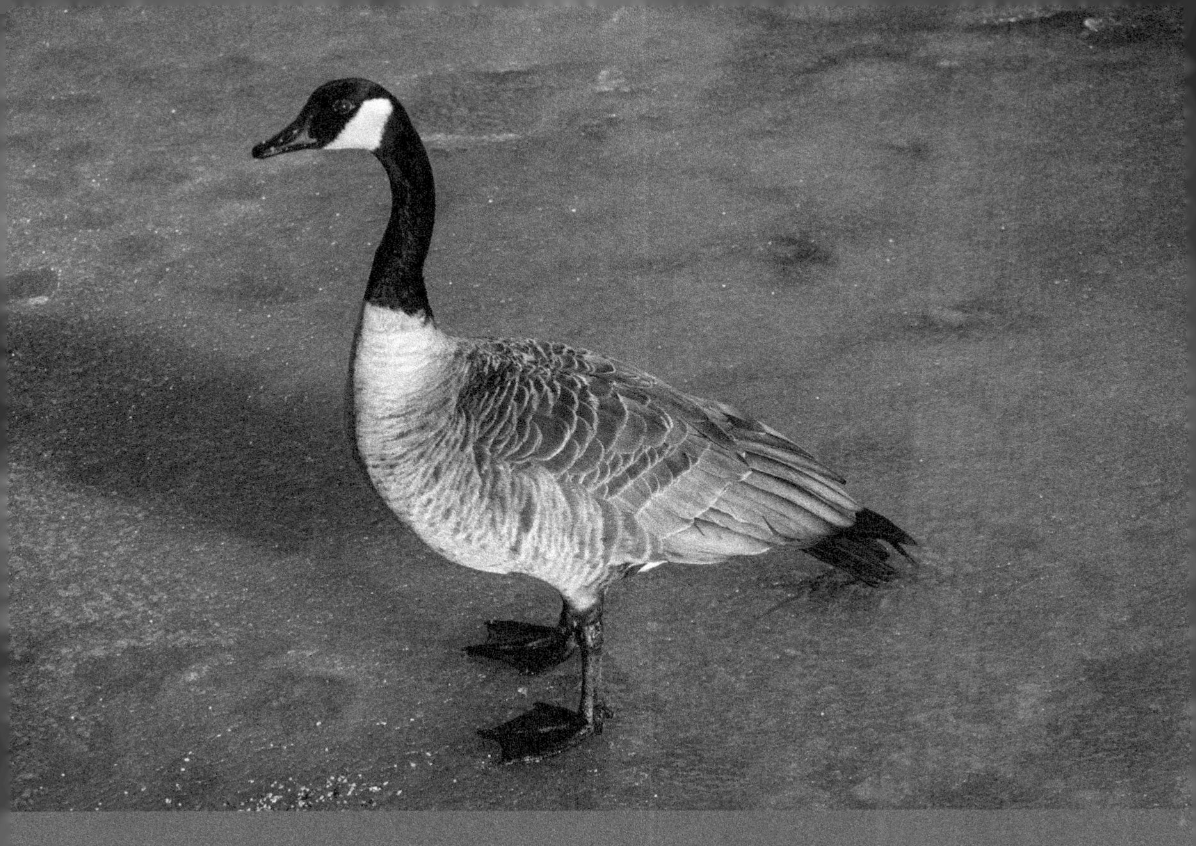

Goose was an introvert, born among extroverts. That gave her certain advantages. Seed was one of them. Humans felt sorry for her and gave her seeds. Before her extroverted cousins saw it, she ate her fill.

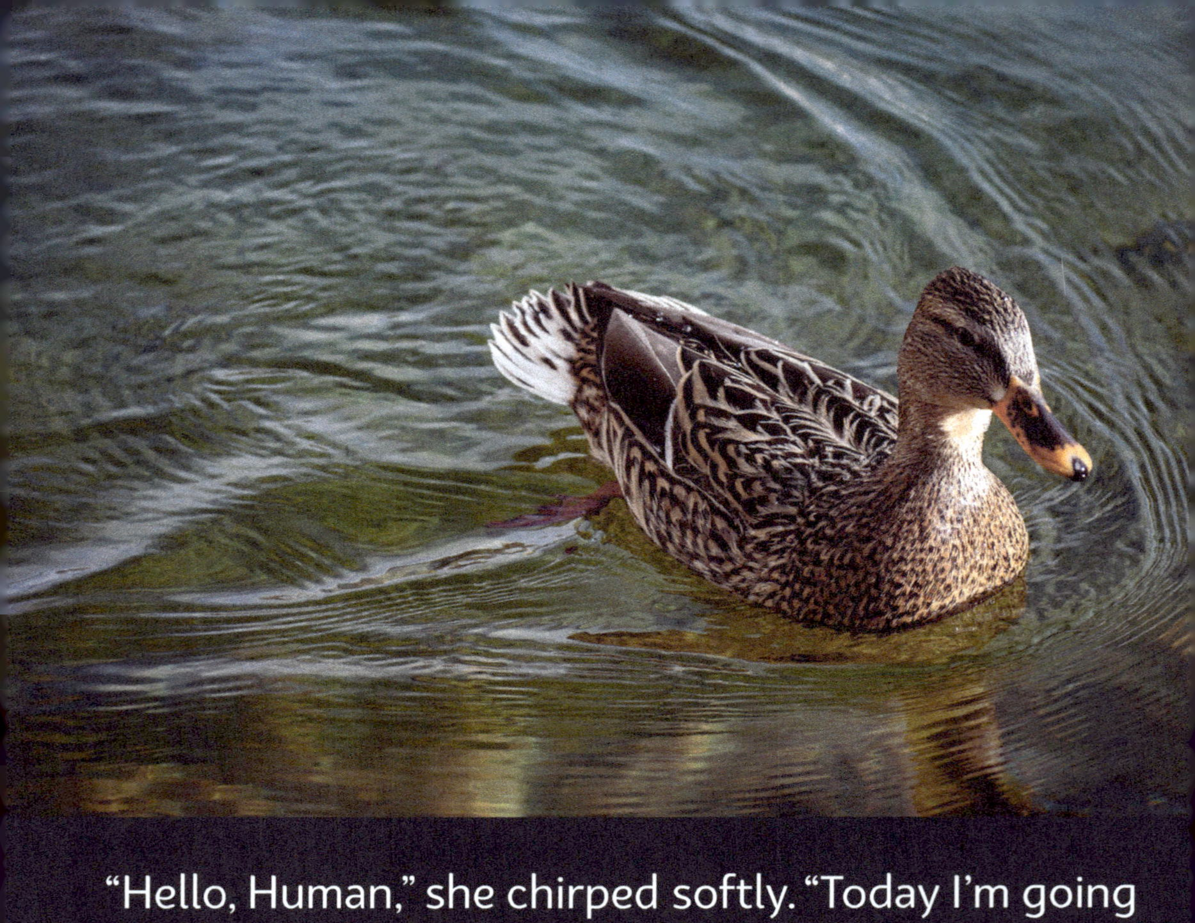

"Hello, Human," she chirped softly. "Today I'm going to surprise you." And she did. She followed the seed bringer, flew to catch up with her, sat beside her and ate out of her hand. The human was charmed.

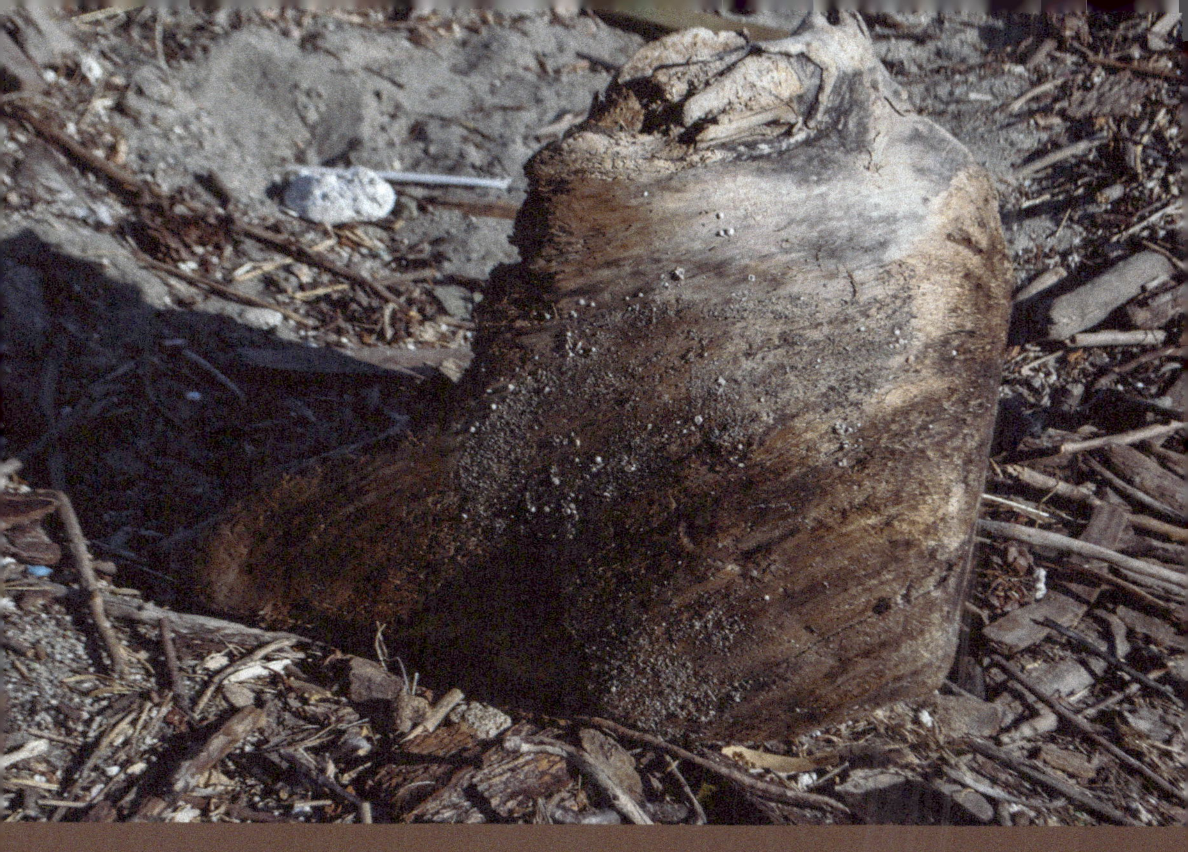

He sat still, shoulders hunched against the wind. It was a long time before he realized the floods had moved him into a sheltered spot, where wind seldom reached. He decided to revise his story, from miserable victim to plucky survivor.

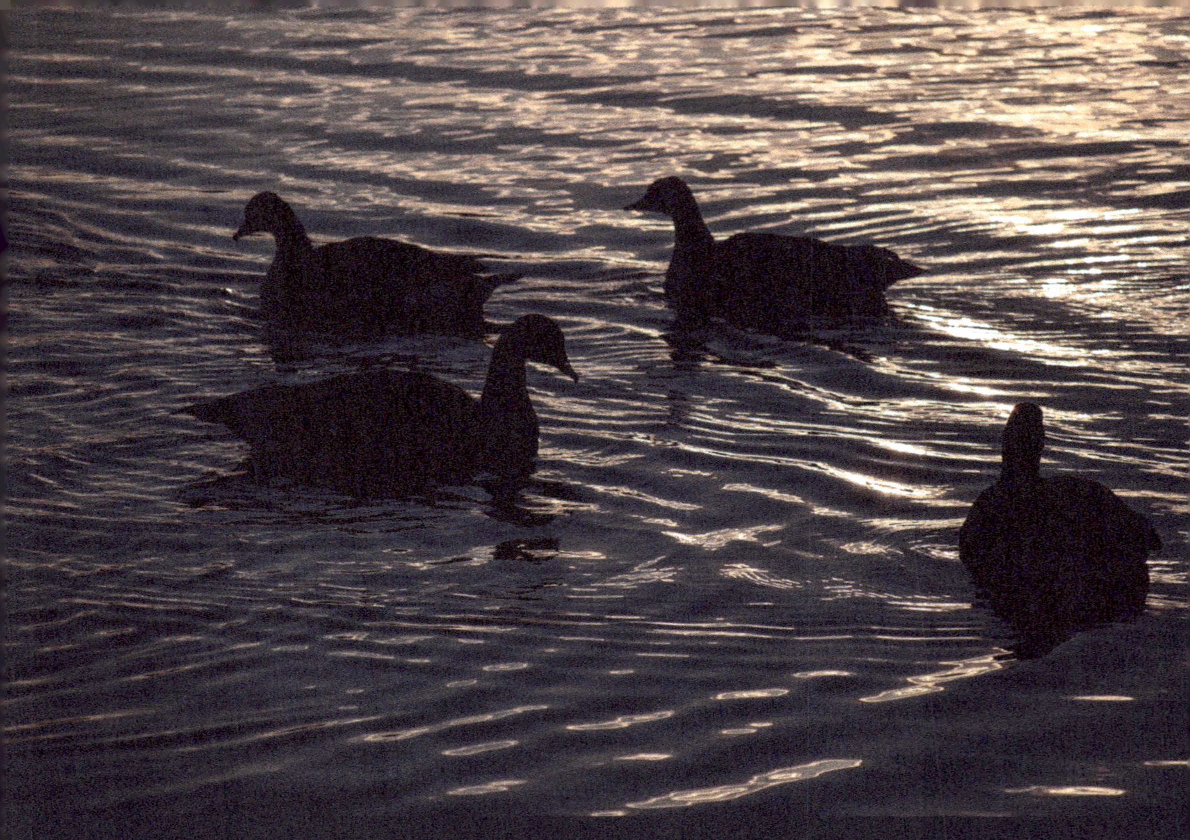

At dusk they met in a circle, each taking a turn to honk about the day. They had found good grass, chased off predators, and come closer to finding this year's nesting sites. Their bellies were full. They were ready for tomorrow's challenges.

ABOUT THE AUTHOR

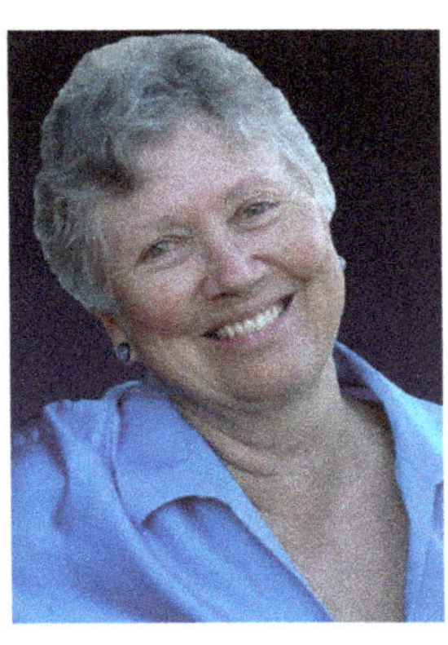

Cathryn Wellner is a writer, photographer and storyteller living in Kelowna, British Columbia, Canada. Her recent books include:

Small Scale Stories series (*That Tree Talked to Me, Parts of Me Are Still Amazing, The Disappearing Pumpkin Choir, In the Shelter of Each Other, Your Task Is to Be Admired, In the Country of Plastic, I'll Tell You a Story, Excited and Kind of Scared, On the Small Side*)

Essay collections (*Hope Wins & Feisty Aging*)
In the Hug of Hills

Millie's Foster Family children's series (*Millie's Feathered Foster Family, Turkey Baby and the Hungry Hawk, Turkey Baby Finds Her Magic*)

You can find links to these and her other books at cathrynwellner.com. Contact her at cathryn@cathrynwellner.com or 778-478-2760. Her photographs can be found on her Web site, as well as on Facebook and Instagram.

BE A BOOK REVIEW ANGEL

If you enjoyed this book, please post a review on Amazon or Goodreads. Share it with friends and rave about it on social media. You can contact the author at cathryn@cathrynwellner.com.

Authors rely on their readers to help spread the word about books they like. People who review books are special kinds of reader angels. I guarantee when you review this book, or any other book that has given you pleasure in any way, you'll feel those wings poking out your back. Look closely in the mirror, and you might even see a halo.

www.ingramcontent.com/pod-product-compliance
Lightning Source LLC
Chambersburg PA
CBHW041051050726
47599CB00018B/2107